Your Personal Revolution

A Weekly Devotional

GARY & DRENDA KEESEE

Your Personal Revolution: A Weekly Devotional
Copyright © 2021 by Gary and Drenda Keesee.

Unless otherwise indicated, all Scriptures are taken from the New International Version® (NIV)® of the Holy Bible. Copyright © 1973, 1978, 1984, 2011 by Biblica, Inc.™ All rights reserved.

Scriptures marked (NLT) are taken from the New Living Translation of the Holy Bible. Copyright © 1996, 2004, 2015 by Tyndale House Foundation. Used by permission of Tyndale House Publishers, Inc., Carol Stream, Illinois 60188. All rights reserved.

Scriptures marked (MSG) are taken from The Message Version of the Holy Bible. Copyright © 1993, 2002, 2018 by Eugene H. Peterson. Used by permission of NavPress. Represented by Tyndale House Publishers, Inc. All rights reserved.

Scriptures marked (ESV) are taken from the ESV® Bible (The Holy Bible, English Standard Version®). ESV® Text Edition: 2016. Copyright © 2001 by Crossway, a publishing ministry of Good News Publishers. All rights reserved.

Scriptures marked (NKJV) are taken from the New King James Version® of the Holy Bible. Copyright © 1982 by Thomas Nelson. All rights reserved.

Scriptures marked (NASB) are taken from the New American Standard Bible®. Copyright © 1960, 1971, 1977, 1995, 2020 by The Lockman Foundation. All rights reserved.

Scriptures marked (EHV) are taken from the Evangelical Heritage Version®, EHV® of the Holy Bible. Copyright © 2019 by the Wartburg Project, Inc. All rights reserved.

Scriptures marked (KJV) are taken from the King James Version of the Holy Bible. Public domain.

Printed in the United States of America. All rights reserved under International Copyright Law. Contents and/or cover may not be reproduced in whole or in part in any form without the express written consent of the Publisher.

ISBN: 978-1-945930-64-5

Published by Free Indeed Publishers.

Distributed by Faith Life Now.

Faith Life Now
P.O. Box 779
New Albany, OH 43054
1-(888)-391-LIFE

You can reach Faith Life Now Ministries on the Internet at www.faithlifenow.com.

CONTENTS

Introduction Your Personal Revolution..................09

Week 1 Get Off the Hamster Wheel..................15

Week 2 Think Big..................23

Week 3 Change Your Allegiance..................31

Week 4 Start with Your Thoughts..................39

Week 5 Don't Disqualify Yourself..................47

Week 6 Get the Right Picture..................55

Week 7 Know This: God Is Good—*Always*..................63

Week 8 Do Unto Others..................71

Week 9 Show God's Heart..................79

Week 10 Dust Yourself Off and Move Forward..................87

Week 11 Find Your Answers in the Kingdom..................95

Week 12 Decide What Success Is to You..................103

Week 13 Believe That You Have Received..................111

Week 14	Have the Right Response	119
Week 15	Get the Instruction You Need	127
Week 16	Break the Curse	135
Week 17	Know Your Legal Rights	143
Week 18	Build on the Rock	151
Week 19	Fund God's Assignment	159
Week 20	Conquer Excuses	167
Week 21	See Yourself as God Does	175
Week 22	Think Right Thoughts	183
Week 23	Seek the Kingdom First	191
Week 24	Complement Each Other	199
Week 25	Ask God for the Plan	207
Week 26	Don't Hand Over the Keys	215
Week 27	Use Your Authority	223
Week 28	Renew Your Mind	231
Week 29	Partner with God	239
Week 30	Don't Be Ruled by Feelings	247
Week 31	Live at Rest	255
Week 32	Communicate Successfully	263
Week 33	Stop Begging God	271

Week 34	Ask Yourself These Questions	279
Week 35	Don't Silence Your Conscience	287
Week 36	Break Up with Fear	295
Week 37	Be Fully Persuaded	303
Week 38	Turn Life's Negatives into Fuel	311
Week 39	Give Your Tithe in Faith	319
Week 40	Make Every Effort to Live in Peace	327
Week 41	Have More Than Enough	335
Week 42	Walk in Confidence	343
Week 43	Enjoy the Kingdom of God	351
Week 44	Clean Out the Junk	359
Week 45	Take Time to Prepare	367
Week 46	Be Teachable	375
Week 47	Look for Opportunities	383
Week 48	Stay Alert	391
Week 49	Set the Measure with a Big Vision	399
Week 50	Fight the Good Fight	407
Week 51	Let Nothing Be Wasted	415
Week 52	Keep Your Peace	423

Introduction
Your Personal Revolution

Introduction

God has great plans for you, friend.

What's holding you back?

What's keeping you from doing what you want to do in life?

What's keeping you from doing what God has called you to do?

If you're like most people, you have at least one reason.

That's way too intimidating. I'm too old. I don't have enough money. I've made too many mistakes. I don't have the right experience to take that on. I'm too young. I'm too shy. I don't have the talent. I don't have what it takes.

The list could go on and on.

We've been there.

Throughout both our lives, we've had all sorts of reasons not to move forward with the things God was calling us to do. In fact, at one time or another, we've probably told ourselves every one of the reasons we just gave you.

But most of those reasons were really just excuses we kept allowing ourselves to make because we were really afraid.

Don't give up on God's incredible plan for your life just

because you're afraid or because you face obstacles or hurdles.

This is your year to win, friend. No matter what month of the year it is right now, real change can start now.

But you're going to have to refuse to settle, back down, or quit.

Of course, we sometimes need to be patient with our aspirations, but most of the time, our problem isn't that we're trying to move things ahead too quickly but that, at some point, we adapted to cope with negative situations in life and then we parked there, or we got stuck in that rut.

We once knew an elderly lady who lived through the very tough times of the Great Depression. I (Drenda) would often see her wearing a pair of tattered gloves. I wanted to bless her, so I bought her a new pair of gloves and took them to her.

After she opened the gift, she took me to her dresser. When she opened the dresser drawer, I was shocked.

Inside the drawer lay SIX other pairs of brand-new gloves. SIX!

She laid the pair I had just given her alongside the other six and closed the drawer.

Introduction

I couldn't believe it. She couldn't use or enjoy any of those gloves because her mind was STUCK. Her fear of not having enough had led her to hold onto nearly everything too tightly. She had developed a wrong pattern of thinking and acting that was holding her back in life.

Just like that pair of gloves, God wants to give YOU good gifts. He wants to promote you. He wants you to win in life.

What's holding you back? What behaviors, habits, and old patterns of thinking and acting are holding you back from being the best you can be and living the life God wants for you?

Friend, we want this to be your year. We want to see you go to the next level with God.

That's why we've compiled 52 of our favorite excerpts from our books—one for every week of the next year—into this one, power-packed study devotional.

Each week features a Bible verse to reflect and meditate on throughout your week, an excerpt from one of our books, a "Prayer Focus," questions to help you "Think on It," and an action step to help you "Pursue Change."

Why "Pursue Change"? Because we know from experience that it's not enough to say you want change; and to think about change, you must pursue change!

YOUR PERSONAL REVOLUTION

So, here it is—your comprehensive collection of teachings, Scriptures, and stories about healings, the promises of God, prayer, provision, overcoming problems, faith, your destiny, and more that you can use as a weekly study devotional—your opportunity to truly pursue not just change but *Your Personal Revolution*.

What is this REVOLUTION? It's a *revolt* against the kingdom of darkness and the system designed to confine you to a life of survival and fear. Because you should be living out your God-designed destiny, a life full of purpose, passion, and hope for your future.

What are you waiting for? You don't have to wait until January 1. Start now.

Know that we love you. You are special to us, and we're praying for you.

It's time to go to the next level with God!

With love,

Gary and Drenda Keesee

Week 1
Get Off the Hamster Wheel

Come to me, all you who are weary and burdened, and I will give you rest. Take my yoke upon you and learn from me, for I am gentle and humble in heart, and you will find rest for your souls. For my yoke is easy and my burden is light.
—Matthew 11:28-30

"As we began to seek God for answers and principles, hope began to rise in our hearts as we saw one miracle after another when we applied what God showed us."
—*Your Financial Revolution: The Power of Rest*

Are you tired? Are you overwhelmed most days and never get caught up? Is your need for money driving your decisions as to where you work or how you work or how long you work? Does it seem that you will never get out of debt? Does it seem you are living the proverbial rat race? If this is you, you are not alone.

Have you ever seen a hamster wheel? I'm sure you have, but in case you have not, it is a wheel that is put in a hamster cage. The hamster can get on that wheel and run and run and run and run until he is worn out. But there is one problem with that wheel. No matter how fast or how long the hamster runs, when he is good and tired and gets off, he is in the exact same place he started from. Nothing has changed. He can wipe the sweat from his furry little face with a satisfied feeling. But nothing was accomplished to benefit his position in life; he is still locked up in a cage with no freedom.

This pretty much sums up many people, if not the majority of people, and their financial lives. They work hard all week and fall exhausted into a brief diversion on the weekend, but when Monday morning comes around, they find themselves in the exact same location as they were the week before. All they have done is survived one more week.

This was a picture of my life for nine long years. I was putting in 15-18 hours a day, I was diligent, and I worked

Week 1: Get Off the Hamster Wheel

hard, but after I paid my tithe, my bills, and taxes, there was nothing left. Creditors were lining up to file against me, and that's when it happened.

The call came in like most other morning calls: "Mr. Keesee, as you know, you owe our client X amount of money. When do you think you can get this to us? Well, Mr. Keesee, you said that the last three times I called you. If you do not have the money to us in three days, my client will be filing a lawsuit for this debt against you. Do you understand, Mr. Keesee? Three days. Goodbye."

The call hit me like a ton of bricks. Not that I already did not know how dire our financial situation was. I had no money. Everything I owned was broken. My refrigerator was empty. My beautiful family was sleeping by the fireplace to keep warm as there was no money for heating oil. I had nowhere to turn. My friends and family were tired of paying my way. Confused, I slowly made my way up the stairs to my bedroom and laid across the bed. I sobbed and cried out to the Lord for help.

I think I was surprised how fast the Lord spoke to me. It was not an audible voice but a voice that suddenly came up out of my spirit and into my mind with force. The first thing the Lord said to me was that the mess I was in had nothing to do with Him. I suppose He said that because I was a little confused as to why He, from my perspective, had not helped us. He said the reason I was in this mess was because I had never learned how His Kingdom operates. He told me that His Kingdom does not operate like the earth realm operates in regard to money, and I would have to learn His Kingdom's system of handling finances if I wanted to be free.

The best way to describe what happened next is to look at a light switch. Walk into a room that is dark and simply flip the switch. Light! You can see. That is what it was like when God began to teach us His Kingdom. It was like someone turned on a light switch, and we could see things that we had never seen before. We began to understand that the Kingdom of God is a government with laws that do not change. We realized that we could learn those laws and tap into God's power and wisdom to create the wealth we needed.

—*Your Financial Revolution: The Power of Rest*

Prayer Focus

Thank God for helping you get off the world's "hamster wheel" and giving you true rest.

Week 1: Get Off the Hamster Wheel

Think on It

→ In what ways do you realize you've been on the world's "hamster wheel," running but not getting anywhere?

→ What needs to change?

→ What do you believe you need to learn and understand about the Kingdom of God in order to live a life of rest?

Pursue Change

This week, be sure to carve out time to pray. Unplug, get off the world's "Hamster Wheel," and get plugged in with Him. Determine what needs to change in your life, and take the first step to making it happen.

Notes

Notes

Week 2
Think Big

Week 2: Think Big

"If you can?" said Jesus. "Everything is possible for one who believes."

—Mark 9:23

"Jesus put dreams inside of you that seem impossible in your ability. God gave you those dreams for a reason. They may seem impossible, but they're not through Christ!"

—Shark Proof

I like to think I'm adventurous, but when the captain told me to jump into the ocean with the sharks circling our boat, I couldn't stop the blood from draining from my face. Is this guy crazy? We were miles from shore, far out on the Pacific Ocean. These weren't tame, aquarium sharks—not that I would have volunteered for that either—these were wild blacktip reef sharks. Let me just emphasize—wild sharks!

They weren't as big or scary as great whites, but even at their small size, the idea seemed crazy. Our boat wasn't sinking. I wasn't jumping into the ocean because I had to. Believe it or not, I had actually signed up to do this!

Gary and I won a trip to Bora Bora through his business a couple of years back. I had always dreamed of going to Bora Bora and staying in a hut on the water. I was thrilled! When we won the trip, we also won a boat trip to swim with stingrays, reef sharks, and lemon sharks while we were there. I didn't plan on swimming with sharks when I said yes to get on the boat, but I'm from the South... We don't turn down free things—it's just not in our nature! So, when I heard they were giving us a FREE BOAT RIDE? No-brainer! Sign me up!

I'll never forget the look on my husband's face when I told him what I had gotten us into. "A friend told me it's amazing," I said. "We'll just ride the boat, and if there's anything we want to do, we can do it."

Week 2: Think Big

After over 30 years of marriage, Gary knew better than to believe that for one second. He looked at me cautiously, knowing as soon as I saw other people having fun swimming with the sharks, I would drag us both in. What can I say? He was right! Nonetheless, I convinced him to get on the boat, and we embarked on one of the biggest adventures of our lives.

Can you think of a time you had to have courage, face a fear, or stand up to a difficult situation? How did you feel after you did it?

If we don't say YES to opportunities, we limit our success… but when we have the courage to wade into the waters with God, our potential is limitless! When we face fear and overcome it, it's *empowering.*

I want you to think BIG. I want you to shut down thoughts of doubt, and let your imagination run wild with your dreams. In order to jump into the water, you need to believe in yourself!

Walt Disney had a system to determine whether he was thinking big enough. After he shared his vision with his team, he'd wait to hear what they had to say. If their response was, "Sure! We can do that!" He knew he wasn't thinking big enough. He'd draw up a new plan and bring it to them. If they told him it sounded impossible, he knew that's what they were going to do.

Jesus put dreams inside of you that seem impossible in your ability. God gave you those dreams for a reason. They may *seem* impossible, but they're not through Christ! That's why Jesus encouraged us, *"'If you can?' said Jesus. 'Everything is possible for one who believes'"* (Mark 9:23).

You may feel like I did that day on the boat, eyeing the beautiful water but scared to jump in because of the sharks. You see the impossibilities, challenges, or difficult people staring you in the face. Maybe you've taken steps toward your destiny in the past, but difficult people have scared you away or tempted you to quit. It's time to let go of everything that's held you back, intimidated you, or discouraged you in the past. It's time to be fearless!

If you're waiting for the perfect opportunity, the perfect training, or the perfect tools before you step out in obedience to God, you'll be waiting forever.

God has a great plan for your life. He wants you to get your hopes up and to dream big, but I would be wrong not to tell you that there are going to be situations that come about which are intended by the enemy to hurt you, bother you, hinder you, and keep you from your destiny... but the journey is worth it.

—Shark Proof

Week 2: Think Big

Prayer Focus

Thank God for giving you dreams and visions for your future and for making anything possible with Him.

Think on It

→ What dreams do you have that seem impossible right now?

→ What would you be doing right now if you knew you couldn't fail?

→ What is one thing you can do in the next week to move one step closer to your dream?

Pursue Change

This week, take at least 10 minutes a day just to dream God-sized dreams—dreams you could never accomplish on your own. It may not come easily. You may have to push yourself, and you may have to dig deep. Pray and ask God for help dreaming His dreams for your life. Then, take action.

Notes

Notes

Week 3
Change Your Allegiance

The blessing of the Lord makes a person wealthy, and he adds no sorrow to it.

—**Proverbs 10:22 (EHV)**

"Stop aligning yourself with all the doubt and unbelief around you. Change your allegiance and enjoy the Kingdom of God!"

—*Your Financial Revolution: The Power of Allegiance*

What you are about to read is a powerful Kingdom principle.

Joseph was hated by his brothers, and they wanted to get rid of him. Actually, they wanted to kill him, but one of the brothers did not want to go that far; so instead, they sold him to some traveling traders who carried him down to Egypt where he was sold to Potiphar, a captain in Pharaoh's guard.

> *Now Joseph had been taken down to Egypt. Potiphar, an Egyptian who was one of Pharaoh's officials, the captain of the guard, bought him from the Ishmaelites who had taken him there. The Lord was with Joseph so that he prospered, and he lived in the house of his Egyptian master. When his master saw that the Lord was with him and that the Lord gave him success in everything he did, Joseph found favor in his eyes and became his attendant. Potiphar put him in charge of his household, and he entrusted to his care everything he owned.*
>
> *From the time he put him in charge of his household and of all that he owned, the Lord blessed the household of the Egyptian because of Joseph. The blessing of the Lord was on everything Potiphar had, both in the house and in the field. So Potiphar left everything he had in Joseph's care; with Joseph in charge, he did not concern himself with anything except the food he ate.*
>
> —Genesis 39:1-6

Week 3: Change Your Allegiance

Pay attention to verse 2a, "*The Lord was with Joseph so that he prospered.*" What does this mean? Is God not with everyone? In the context of what we have been discussing in previous chapters regarding lineage, the answer is no. Remember, Abraham's faith and the covenant that followed gave God legal access to Abraham and his heirs—only. So when we are talking about God being with everyone, it is not to be confused with God loving everyone; He does. But for those without a legal standing before God, His hands are tied.

> *Remember that at that time you were separate from Christ, excluded from citizenship in Israel and foreigners to the covenants of the promise, without hope and without God in the world. But now in Christ Jesus you who once were far away have been brought near by the blood of Christ.*
> —Ephesians 2:12-13

Notice this Scripture talks about being without covenant, meaning that God and His power are legally cut off from a person. Why? Because God does not have the legality or jurisdiction in the earth realm without a legal agreement, a covenant in place, with a man or woman on the earth. This verse plainly brings this out when it says that without a covenant, people are without hope and without God in the world. Remember that since Jesus put a new covenant in place for us, we are now members of God's own household and citizens of His great Kingdom (Ephesians 2:19.) So now, looking back at our Scripture in Genesis 39, we understand the phrase "*The Lord was with Joseph*" meant that legally, God had influence in Joseph's life through the covenant that his grandfather Abraham had put in place. This legal covenant, allowing God's blessing and influence, overrode the earth realm's painful toil and sweat system. It was legal for God to bless Joseph.

Remember what God said to Abraham earlier, "*I will make you.*" Because God was with Joseph, helping him in life, he had success in everything he did, so much so that his heathen master, Potiphar, saw a huge difference in Joseph's ability compared to the many other men he had seen. I should mention here that when we prosper with God's help, the people who are living under the earth curse system of survival notice the difference! Potiphar was so impressed that he put Joseph in charge of his entire estate.

I want you to get a clear picture of what is happening here. One day Joseph was not in charge, and the next he was. The Bible makes note of a moment in time when that change occurred. The blessing of the Lord came on all of Potiphar's stuff, his entire estate! But he did not know the God of Joseph and was not part of the nation of Israel. So how could this happen, and what does it mean? Here's the answer. When Potiphar put his estate under the authority of Joseph, without knowing it, his estate came under the covenant that Joseph had with God.

Week 3: Change Your Allegiance

Potiphar's stuff, his estate, and property all changed kingdoms!!

—*Your Financial Revolution: The Power of Allegiance*

Prayer Focus

Thank God for giving you a clear picture of His promises to us through Joseph's story—His promise to be with you wherever you go and His promise that you can be successful at whatever you put your hands to with His help.

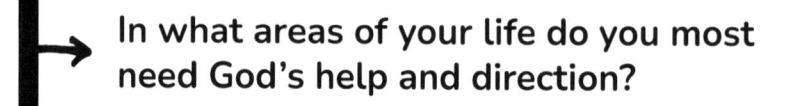

Think on It

> In what areas of your life do you most need God's help and direction?

> What are the areas of your life where you know you have not trusted God?

> Have you ever asked God for His plan for your life? If so, what did He say? If not, why?

Pursue Change

Ephesians 3:20 tells us God is able to do more than all you ask or imagine, according to His power that is at work within you. This week, determine that you are going to trust God and step into His plan for your life. Make a list of at least five areas of your life, and find specific Scripture declarations to speak over those areas daily.

Notes

Notes

Week 4
Start with Your Thoughts

Week 4: Start with Your Thoughts

The mind governed by the flesh is death, but the mind governed by the Spirit is life and peace.

—Romans 8:6

"Your success story begins with a change in your thoughts—when you learn to think right, you can literally think your way to success!"

—Better Than You Think

I've discovered that people from all walks of life want a key to success. They want a five-step program that assures them of quick, fail-safe results to make them more popular, beautiful, wealthy, and happy; and the culture is eager to sell it to them at top dollar.

Unfortunately, most of the culture sells empty promises of overnight success: get-rich-quick schemes, fad diets to lose 10 pounds in 10 days, magazines advertising 21 steps to make any man fall in love with you, a lottery ticket to become an overnight millionaire, and many more... There are real solutions for you, but the culture's gimmicks are not your answer!

Do you think the shade of lipstick or the kind of shoes you wear are going to make you happy or more successful? They might make you feel good for a moment, but when that moment runs out, you'll be searching for new promises to buy into and more temporary happiness to give you a moderately satisfying life. That is why people that rely on material things to give them an identity are always searching and always trying to find more to satisfy themselves.

When people reach the world's standard of success apart from God, they still find themselves depressed, tired, and hurting because their success is founded on the wrong things. They're busy and rundown by the uphill struggle. Families go into hundreds of thousands of dollars of debt to keep up with the Joneses, but it's still not enough. Maybe

Week 4: Start with Your Thoughts

if they had nicer houses or newer cars, or more money, then they would be happy? But they're not! Since their success is based upon the wrong groundwork, it only magnifies the turmoil on the inside of them and creates more pressure.

God placed a desire in you for success and happiness. He created you with the innate hunger to find out what you were crafted to do and to succeed at it. That is why those cheap promises of success the culture sells are so appealing—they mimic the promises of God. You were born asking, "Who am I?" and the culture is communicating on hundreds of media platforms, "This is who you are."

It's easy to get caught up in what the loudest voice tells you success should look like and how it should feel. You were designed to look to God for your identity and your answers, not to the culture. As long as you trust the culture to give you something it can't give—happiness, love, value, purpose—you will always be disappointed!

> *Do not conform to the pattern of this world, but be transformed by the renewing of your mind. Then you will be able to test and approve what God's will is—His good, pleasing and perfect will.*
> —Romans 12:2

Your success can't exist apart from God. It starts with God, His Word, and your thoughts. That is the key. Success comes from inside of you, from your attitude, from your perspective on life, and works its way out.

> "Our thoughts become our WORDS.
> Our words become our ACTIONS.
> Our actions become our HABITS.
> Our habits become our CHARACTER.
> Our character determines our DESTINY."
> —Gandhi

Your success story begins with a change in your thoughts—when you learn to think right, you can literally think your way to success!

You may believe that the term "thinking right" is a little vague, unattainable, or even impossible. What do we base right and wrong on anyway? There has been some debate about that, which is why we see the nation in the mess it's in now. But "thinking right" isn't as complicated as it sounds. The word "right" is a result of righteousness, or the "right way" to do something—God's way. You find righteousness when you seek God. He has given you the amazing gift of salvation, but that is only the beginning! God has made a way for you to live in success. He has given you His Word to help you see the way He sees.

The Creator of the Universe sacrificed His Son for your salvation. Salvation means welfare, prosperity, deliverance,

Week 4: Start with Your Thoughts

preservation, health, wholeness, and safety. All of those things are a part of your inheritance. Jesus paid the price for you to live successfully in every area. If your spirit is alive to God, then salvation (and all that encompasses) is yours!

God has the real fail-safe plan for success in your life. He doesn't rely on empty promises and sales gimmicks. He has a genuine program to give you real results in your life—results of confidence, beauty, peace, wealth, and fulfillment.

The key to walking in your full potential is to tap into the amazing ability to see life through God's perspective.

—*Better Than You Think*

Prayer Focus

Ask God to reveal any and every thought that has been holding you back from living the life He has for you.

Think on It

→ What have you been thinking recently?

→ Do you choose what you think about, or do you allow yourself to think on anything that pops up in your mind?

→ What excuses do you give yourself for not reading the Word of God?

Pursue Change

This week, practice testing every thought you have against God's will for you. How do you know His will? It's made known to us in His Word, the Bible. Measure everything against what God says in His Word. Umpire your thoughts. If they don't line up with what God says, get them out! Replace them with right thoughts.

Notes

Week 5
Don't Disqualify Yourself

can also be trusted with much, and whoever is dishonest with very little will also be dishonest with much. So if you have not been trustworthy in handling worldly wealth, who will trust you with true riches? And if you have not been trustworthy with someone else's property, who will give you property of your own?

—Luke 16:10-12

"If Satan can remove all respect for authority and convince everyone that they can do whatever they please when they please, then the world will collapse into chaos and ruin."
—*Your Financial Revolution: The Power of Strategy*

Today, everyone wants to have authority without being under authority, and that is impossible.

Last week, I talked to a woman who said that she did not need a pastor; it was just her and the Holy Spirit. Really? Well, she had better go and talk to Jesus about that because He is the One who appointed pastors and set up the local church in Ephesians chapter 4. If she is submitted to Jesus, then she will follow the authority that Jesus set up. The fact is she is not submitted to Jesus and wants to do her own thing. She will most likely fall into deception and hard times because of it.

Not too long ago, I talked to a salesperson who was starting their own sales company and was taking all of their clients from their company with them, even though they had signed a non-compete agreement stating that they would not do that. And they think that they will prosper in doing that? That is simply stealing!

I know that you may not like this chapter as much as the others where I laid out the supernatural, cool stuff the Holy Spirit does, but if you do not get this chapter right, you might as well forget all the rest because it is God who promotes.

I remember the time a woman came up to me at a prayer meeting and was in tears, asking me why I did not call on her to pray. I was shocked! Why was it such a big deal to

Week 5: Don't Disqualify Yourself

be called upon to pray unless, of course, her identity was based on being seen by men?

And, of course, I could have told her why I did not call on her in a minute if she would have ever listened to anyone. This woman did not respect her husband and was constantly putting his lack of spirituality down in the gossip sessions she was always involved with. That is why I did not call on her. The fact that she came up in tears because she was not seen as the spiritual woman she thought she was before the whole group revealed that she did not respect authority and, thus, was a dangerous woman.

So let me ask you a question. Are you qualified to go where you want to go, where your dreams want to go? If I asked your pastor or your boss what their honest opinion of you was, what would they say? You see, you cannot have authority until you pass the submission test. I did not say this; Jesus did.

Can you be trusted with authority? The evidence is in your submission.

Let's take a look at a story in the Bible which could have a profound bearing on the success you have in life.

In 1 Samuel 13:13-14, we see Saul was disqualified because he did not submit to authority. So again we see if you cannot submit to authority, you cannot have authority.

I want to make a very important point here. The Lord was going to search out a man after his own heart. What does "after his own heart" mean?"

> *After removing Saul, he made David their king. He testified concerning him: "I have found David son of Jesse, a man after my own heart; he will do everything I want him to do."*
> —Acts 13:22

How does God define someone who has His heart? Basically, it is someone who hates what God hates and loves what God loves, someone who will do what God would have done if He were there. In other words, if God hates sin, they hate sin. If God wants to get something done, they want to get it done. In our world, we think someone after God's own heart is someone who has the most spiritual gifting. We think being spiritual is soft worship music. But God clearly says that being obedient is spiritual worship.

—*Your Financial Revolution: The Power of Strategy*

Prayer Focus

Thank God for the authorities in your life, regardless of how you have felt about them up until this point. Then pray for them.

Week 5: Don't Disqualify Yourself

Think on It

→ How well do you follow instructions from someone in authority?

→ When your leader gives you something to do that you don't really want to do, how do you act?

→ Is there any authority in your life that you need to forgive?

Pursue Change

This week, make sure you're not stuck in any of the stages of disloyalty in any area of your life. Do you have an independent spirit, constantly wanting to do things your way? Are you offended? Have you stopped engaging in an area? Are you critical? Have you tried to draw others to your "side"? Are you in open rebellion against a leader in your life? It's never too late to change. Make the choice to be loyal, obedient, and submissive to God and, therefore, to the leaders He has placed in your life. Forgive and move forward.

Notes

Notes

Week 6
Get the Right Picture

"When we meditate on God's picture, it produces hope and faith in our hearts until the picture on the inside of us matches what God says. You'll believe what God says. You'll expect what God says. And you'll begin to see what God says become a reality in your life."

—*Better Than You Feel*

It is for freedom that Christ has set you free. You weren't called to a life of bondage to your soul with its appetites, lusts, and emotional baggage. You were created with potential. You have a heart full of treasures—the desires, feelings, talents, and unique traits that make you a special individual.

What are you doing with them?

KEYS TO WINNING

RIGHT PICTURE
Concept: Faith
Source: God's Word

"Change the Picture"

MORE POWER
Concept: Grace
Source: God's Spirit

"Receive the Power"

We can become buried in life's difficulties if we don't learn how to master our emotions and will. That mastery is never completely realized without God's power working on our behalf by His Spirit. His Word brings us the picture of faith, but it's His power that brings self-control and the rest of the fruit of the Spirit in our lives.

We need the picture, which is painted for us in the Word of God, but we also need the power to carry it out. That's

Week 6: Get the Right Picture

called grace—the ability of God—working on our behalf. I can have the picture, and it will produce faith that it is possible, but the Spirit of God gives me the power to overcome my fleshly appetites and the nagging reminders of my past limitations and insecurities.

When we meditate on God's picture, it produces hope and faith in our hearts until the picture on the inside of us matches what God says. You'll believe what God says. You'll expect what God says. And you'll begin to see what God says become a reality in your life. When God's picture is in you, and His power is on you, you can do all things through Christ!

One of the worst things you can die with is wasted potential! Ask yourself, "Am I using my potential? What is holding me back from using my potential?"

The Three Areas That Dictate Our Actions:

Mind: your mental outlook, mindset, or belief system

Will: your choices, priorities, and desires

Emotions: your feelings, attitudes, and reactions to circumstances based on your mindset and desires

Many people are sick and weak because their bodies are reflecting what's in their soul realm. Instead of looking to

God, people allow themselves to become convinced of their identity outside of God's Word.

We can find our identity in God, but if we don't continuously renew our minds with the truth, we forget what the mirror of the Word says. We forget who we are and what we're capable of. It's not enough to know what God's promises say; we must choose to let our faith in those promises lead or rule our lives instead of our will or emotions.

We can miss our purpose if we let our feelings direct our actions. When we realize who we are in Christ and what we have in Him, we discover what we can do and how we should do it.

Colossians 1:16 says, "*Everything got started in HIM and finds its purpose in HIM*" (MSG).

When we sync up with God, we discover our purpose. We find our part in "His" story! People who made a lasting contribution to history or became world changers harnessed their emotions to work for them and not against them. Their purpose became greater than the day-to-day troubles and the emotions, pains of rejection, failure, and disappointments that came along the way. They rose to their purpose, coupled with their emotions, to meet the challenge at hand. They learned to let their emotions energize them but not control them. There's a powerful difference.

—Better Than You Feel

Week 6: Get the Right Picture

Prayer Focus

Ask God to help you harness your emotions and help you to make them work for you and not against you.

Think on It

→ Are you using your God-given potential? How so or why not?

→ Which of the three areas that dictate our actions do you struggle with the most?

→ How often do you allow your feelings to dictate your actions?

Pursue Change

This week, meditate on the following Scripture and sanctify your emotions and feelings by submitting them to God; set them apart; clean them up; manage them as God would, so they can propel you toward your destiny the way He intended them to.

> *May God himself, the God of peace, sanctify you through and through. May your whole spirit, soul and body be kept blameless at the coming of our Lord Jesus Christ.*
> —1 Thessalonians 5:23

Notes

Notes

Week 7
Know This: God Is Good—Always

Week 7: Know This: God Is Good—*Always*

Don't be deceived, my dear brothers and sisters. Every good and perfect gift is from above, coming down from the Father of the heavenly lights, who does not change like shifting shadows.

—James 1:16-17

"Without any wavering or doubt, know that God is good and His Word is truth."

—*Your Financial Revolution: The Power of Provision*

As Drenda and I began to see the Kingdom of God operate in our lives, many times, we were shocked by what we saw. We realized that the majority of believers had no idea how it worked.

For instance, I just read a headline of a seven-year-old that died on the operating table during a tonsillectomy. Though an extremely common and usually very safe operation, her heart just stopped during the operation, an extremely grievous outcome. I think all of our hearts sighed a bit just hearing that it happened. However, as tragic as the event was, there was another tragic part of the story that could affect this family for the rest of their lives. Let me quote what the father said to the reporter, and I am quoting here.

> "You don't understand why these things happen, but we know it was God's plan. And that's the only thing that can get us through, because we know it was God."[1]

Let me also quote Green Bay Packers' quarterback Aaron Rodgers, whose story appeared in *People* magazine on January 22nd, 2020.

> Rodgers explained that he questioned religion as a kid and has since related to a "different type of spirituality" as he's gotten older. "Most people that

---

[1] https://nypost.com/2020/02/26/7-year-old-south-carolina-girl-dies-during-tonsillectomy.

> I knew, church was just ... you just had to go." He also said, "I don't know how you can believe in a God who wants to condemn most of the planet to a fiery hell. What type of loving, sensitive, omnipresent, omnipotent being wants to condemn his beautiful creation to a fiery hell at the end of all this?"[2]

Crazy comments! But if this is what they believe about God, you would have to agree, who could trust or desire to serve a God that wanted to take their seven-year-old daughter? No one! And who wants to serve a God who "wants" to condemn most of the planet to hell? No one! But that is what the majority of Christians believe. You have heard it all your life: "God allowed it," "God did it," "It was God's plan," "It was their time to go," and many more statements like that. In fact, I am going to bet that you probably think the same way. So I am going to be blunt. If you really believe that God is like that, that He would willingly kill a child or give someone cancer, then we need to have a serious talk.

Let me say it this way: **YOU WILL NEVER BELIEVE SOMEONE YOU DON'T TRUST!**

If you have been taught to distrust God, that He kills innocent people, and if you agree that He is the all-powerful Creator of the universe, then we had better all just do our best to stay on His good side.

---

[2] https://people.com/sports/aaron-rodgers-opens-up-about-religion-to-danica-patrick-i-dont-know-how-you-can-believe-in-a-god.

This is what people did in the past in many primitive cultures. They would make all kinds of offerings to appease the God of wrath. They would put themselves under all kinds of restrictions, even submitting to various kinds of pain, to show they were truly submitted to Him and, hopefully, avoid His wrath. But is this really the character of the God of the Bible? Are we to live in fear of God? No, of course not. The concept that God is against us or not trustworthy is all a result of bad teaching that began in the Garden with Adam and Eve.

Satan has been casting doubts on God's character since time began. Strangely, Eve already had any wisdom she may have felt she was lacking through her relationship with God, Himself. Yet Satan was able to convince her that there was something she was missing that God was withholding from her. Adam and Eve believed a lie about God and willingly cast aside their positions in His Kingdom to pursue a different kingdom. They believed that Satan had a better future for them. Of course, their decision only brought pain, sorrow, and death.

Satan's tactics have never changed, and it is not surprising that his greatest target is the church itself. Because the church already has the authority to put Satan under its feet and defeat him on every front, his only weapons are as they were then: deception and lies.

—Your Financial Revolution: The Power of Provision

Week 7: Know This: God Is Good—*Always*

Prayer Focus

Thank God that every good and perfect gift is from Him and that He does not change.
(James 1:16-17).

Think on It

→ What do you really believe about God and His character?

→ Do you believe God is good and that He works in all things for your good?

→ Do you believe God's promises are for you?

Pursue Change

This week, meditate on James 1:16-17 as well as the following Scripture, and know that God doesn't change depending on the situation; His character will never change; He is ALWAYS good; you can trust Him. What you believe about God and His character sets the stage for your personal revolution.

And we know that in all things God works for the good of those who love him, who have been called according to his purpose.
—Romans 8:28

Notes

Notes

Week 8
Do Unto Others

Bear with each other and forgive one another if any of you has a grievance against someone. Forgive as the Lord forgave you.

—**Colossians 3:13**

"Nobody is perfect. Remember, you make mistakes, too, so respond to others with the same grace you would like them to extend to you. Forgive quickly and laugh often."

—*Nasty Gets Us Nowhere*

Recently, I had to be away from Gary while ministering in Puerto Rico. My women's ministry, Happy Life, hosted a neighborhood carnival event after hurricanes had ravaged the area. We secured enough Christmas presents to make several hundred children very happy and distributed them at the carnival.

Just before the carnival began, I received a call from our home alarm system that a fire was detected at our house. I knew Gary was supposed to be home, but the security company wasn't able to reach him. Then I remembered that he might be deer hunting, so I told the company that they should dispatch the fire department. Two fire trucks and an ambulance took off for our Georgian-style country home on 60 acres.

I was concerned and prayed, but I needed to focus on the children's party. Later, I received a text from Gary that all was well; he had simply started to cook his breakfast and left it to simmer while he stepped outside to hang up his deer. He didn't realize the simmer setting was hot enough to burn the food.

The kids' party was a hit, and I had the opportunity to bring the Sunday message at the local church we collaborated with to bless the kids. It was a great weekend, and I couldn't wait to get home.

I arrived at 6:30 a.m. after a connection and a few hours

Week 8: Do Unto Others

of sleep. Gary picked me up, and we were elated to see each other and get breakfast together. Although tired, with a new surge of energy, I began my overdue Christmas shopping. Christmas was only a week away! We kept going until we could go no more and finally arrived home at about 5:00 p.m.

Something was wrong.

The house smelled like smoke. *That was it! Gary's fire!*

I had forgotten. Gary detailed again the story of how he wasn't gone long and just didn't think a low-simmering pan would start a fire so quickly. The house had a horrible scorched smell, and I couldn't help but feel agitated about the near disaster.

"I can't believe you almost caught our house on fire! I better not leave you home alone again," I teased. He was embarrassed, and I knew it, but I thought it was a good lesson to school him, my motherly punishment.

The rest of the evening, I searched for ways to get the smell out of our house. Several websites suggested boiling white vinegar with water, so that's what I did. The following morning, I did it again, but our house still reeked with that awful, smoky smell. Imagine the horrible smell of burnt popcorn, except it's in every room of your house.

Later, while I was getting my nails done, my nail technician asked if anything exciting had happened that week. I began to tell her about Gary's pan fire. (I don't make it a practice to share my husband's mistakes, but this was still very much on my mind.)

Fire! Suddenly, I had an epiphany! *I* had left a pan of boiling vinegar on the stove! Almost two hours ago!

In a panic, I started to hyperventilate as I told my nail tech what happened. She quickly wrapped up my session, and I took off in a mad dash to get home. I drove 75 mph with my flashers on, praying frantically and driving like a madwoman. I could just see the fire department at my house again for the second time in one week.

I tried to pray instead of worry. A whirl of thoughts tried to capture me as I drove insanely. "Thank You, God, I will make it in time and our house will not be on fire!"

My goal was to get there not only before a fire started but also before the alarms sounded and the fire department was dispatched. I came flying into our driveway, ran into the hazy, smoky kitchen, leaving the door open, threw open a window, grabbed the charred pan off the stove, and quickly threw it out the window. It bounced off the hot tub cover and rolled down the yard. I ran around, opened the front door, and held my breath, hoping the alarm wouldn't go off.

Week 8: Do Unto Others

Silence. No alarm. All was quiet except for the wind that whisked through the house. I had made it! No fire trucks. No paramedics. No damage.

Except the house smelled worse than ever. Then it hit me: I had done the same thing Gary did. I almost burned the house down. I had shamed him a bit for something I myself was now guilty of...

Isn't it always easier to blame someone else instead of looking at ourselves? Taking personal responsibility for our own contribution to the problem requires humility, but it's the key to resolution.

—Nasty Gets Us Nowhere

Prayer Focus

Ask God for forgiveness and to help you forgive others as He has forgiven you.

Think on It

→ In what relationship in your life are you least likely to take personal responsibility? Why?

→ Do you have a difficult time saying you're sorry?

→ Have you ever allowed hurt feelings to destroy a relationship?

Pursue Change

This week, pray and ask God to help you see any relationship issues you have through His eyes. He has a great way of minimizing offenses and helping us see where we have contributed to problems, even when we think we're innocent. Pray and then choose to forgive just as God chose to forgive us through Jesus.

Once you choose to forgive by faith in the work of Jesus, you'll have a right mind and heart toward the other person. If you need to talk a situation out, then the Holy Spirit will show you how to go about it in a spirit of love and will also tell you when it's the right time to do so.

Notes

Week 9

Show God's Heart

Now he who supplies seed to the sower and bread for food will also supply and increase your store of seed and will enlarge the harvest of your righteousness. You will be enriched in every way so that you can be generous on every occasion, and through us your generosity will result in thanksgiving to God.

—2 Corinthians 9:10-11

"People needed to know the laws of the Kingdom and why giving is such a vital part of walking in the Kingdom's abundance here in the earth realm. And again, more importantly, they needed to know what to do after they gave. They needed to know how to harvest what they needed from God."

—*Your Financial Revolution: The Power of Generosity*

Our family was eating dinner one night at one of our favorite local restaurants. The waitress was a young lady who was very pregnant. As I was about to pay our bill, I suddenly felt led to give her a big tip instead of the 22-25% I usually give, so I added $100 to the tip amount. She picked up the signed Visa slip without looking at it and walked back toward the kitchen.

In a minute, she was back, with tears streaming down her face. She came back to thank us. She told us how she was in a tight financial situation and was wondering how she could make it. We had the opportunity to share Christ with her and pray with her before we left. We did nothing but be generous to open the door of ministry to her heart.

Being generous is acting like God does.

God is good, and He is generous! We are His children, and our new nature in Christ is one of being generous as well. As in the story above, being generous is sharing God's heart for people. Like taking a sip of cold water on a very hot day, being generous brings relief and hope to a world that is in the desert of poverty.

It is part of your duty on God's behalf, here in the earth realm, to share His heart and concern for people. The result is clear—it touches people's hearts and opens them up to receive Christ.

Week 9: Show God's Heart

I think we can all remember when someone came to our aid and how much it meant to us.

I can remember owing $4,000 in taxes when I was first married and having no idea where I would get the money. I lay awake many nights dreading the situation I was in. We lived in Tulsa at the time and had planned to visit Ohio for the holidays.

When my dad asked me how things were going, I told him about the IRS bill. He said, "Well, that is easy to fix," and he pulled out a check and wrote it to me for the entire amount. His instant generosity to me at that moment caused me to love my dad even more than I did. For in that moment, I saw his heart for me.

My dad often kept his heart hidden. He never really showed his emotions openly to people, not even to my mom. My dad had never told me he loved me my entire life up until that point, as far as I could remember. Only once when my mother told him to say it did he finally say it, and after much drama. I can remember that day like it was yesterday. Mom was pleading with him, saying, "You cannot tell your own son that you love him?" But he remained quiet.

Finally, with my mom in tears, he told me he loved me. But I never counted that one moment in time as him telling me he loved me because he was coerced to do so.

Instead of telling us verbally that he loved us, there were times when my dad would buy us something special, and I think all four of us children knew that Dad loved us. I would only see Dad's heart by what he did, almost never by what he said. I held those moments dear as they stood out like lights in a dark night to me.

The day he wrote the check for the IRS debt, my heart was filled with gratitude. In tears, I hugged my dad and thanked him. His response caught me off guard. He said, "As long as I have it, I want to help."

I am sure you have memories of someone's generosity like I do, moments that caught your attention. So, make this mental note: Generosity shows people your heart and God's heart for them.

—*Your Financial Revolution: The Power of Generosity*

Prayer Focus

Thank God that He is faithful and that when you make a deposit into His Kingdom business of people, you always get a return.

Week 9: Show God's Heart

Think on It

> When was the last time you were generous?

> When was the last time someone was generous toward you?

> What would it take for you to "be generous on every occasion"?

Pursue Change

This week, be more aware than ever that you bear God's Name wherever you go. Pay attention to people, and meet their needs when led to by the Holy Spirit. Remember: When you're generous, you touch people on His behalf. And because God is good, He gives seed to the sower; He funds His agenda. As He finds you faithful, He's going to increase your seed.

Notes

Notes

Week 10

Dust Yourself Off and Move Forward

If it is possible, as far as it depends on you, live at peace with everyone.

—Romans 12:18

"The secret is great leaders don't allow failure to REDEFINE their purpose—they use failure to REFINE their purpose."

—*Shark Proof*

One of the hardest lessons Gary and I had to learn in business was noble failure. I *hated* the word failure. I was a straight A student in high school, President of my class, and voted most likely to succeed. My identity came from my accomplishments. I was terrified of failing. I thought if I did, people would retract their love from me. Because of this toxic but extremely common mindset, I was intimidated by the dreams inside of me.

What if people didn't like me? What if I looked stupid? What if I took a risk and fell flat on my face?

There was a powerful lesson that I had to learn before I could fearlessly pursue my dreams.

Nothing equips you for success like NOBLE FAILURE.

I know, I know, it seems like an oxymoron, but it's not! Gary and I learned this lifesaving revelation at our lowest point in ministry. We had issues with our staff and with people in our church congregation, and, honestly, we were ready to throw in the towel and give up on ourselves and people.

In addition to carrying too much responsibility in the ministry, we were allowing sharks in our lives to discourage and manipulate us. We were constantly jumping through hoops for people we thought had our best interests at heart, only to find ourselves disappointed over and over again by betrayal.

Week 9: Dust Yourself Off and Move Forward

After years of these toxic patterns, I had never seen Gary so discouraged and worn down. One day, he came to me with tears in his eyes.

"I wrote my resignation letter today," he said, trying to fight back the crushing disappointment in his voice.

My heart sank.

I knew the situation was dire. We were on the brink of surrendering everything God had called us to do under the weight of hopelessness.

I couldn't help but ask myself: *Why? If God had called us to do ministry, why was it so hard? Why were we waking up with dread and heaviness instead of the excitement and vision we used to have?*

I have seen too many business leaders, dreamers, and spiritual visionaries surrender their God-given assignments because they didn't have the knowledge we learned—the principles that equipped us to stop surviving around sharks and start thriving around them.

That's when God brought an incredible mentor into our lives, Dr. Dean Radtke. He began to encourage us and teach us many leadership principles that radically changed our lives, but one of the most important principles we needed to understand as leaders was the concept of noble failure.

Whether you fail or succeed at something doesn't alter the identity or purpose God placed in you. When you realize that, you don't have to look at failure through hurt, fear, or offense. Every successful person has failed before! Failure doesn't mean you missed your purpose. Failure isn't the daunting, taboo word we often make it out to be. Albert Einstein once said, "Anyone who has never made a mistake has never tried anything new."

He was right! Here's the kicker. When we were children, we were actually encouraged to fail every day. You don't remember that? Maybe that's because it was given a different name. Can you guess what that was?

We called it PRACTICE! Practice is failing at something again and again until we start to fail at it less, and, eventually, don't fail at it at all.

So why, when we're adults, do we begin to look at noble failure as the enemy of our dreams instead of the pathway to our promotion?

Maybe it's because our failures become more visible the older we get. We think people expect us to have it all together, or we think our failure will disqualify us from our destinies. Perhaps our failures confirm the insecurities we have in ourselves, or, out of pride, we want to make people think we have it all together. I don't know why failure becomes this looming "F" word as we get older, but I do

Week 9: Dust Yourself Off and Move Forward

know this: If we are unwilling to risk failure, we must be willing to sacrifice greatness.

> *"I have not failed. I've just found 10,000 ways that won't work."*
>
> —Thomas A. Edison

Noble failure is simply when we do our best, try something new, and it doesn't work out the way we hoped. It's good intentions with a bad outcome. We can learn from noble failure when we dust ourselves off and move forward wiser and better equipped for success!

—*Shark Proof*

Prayer Focus

Thank God that He wants to advance His Kingdom in the earth through you and that He has already prepared a way for you to go and succeed.

Think on It

→ When was the last time you failed at something?

→ Do you make a habit of rehearsing your failures or of moving forward?

→ Have you ever asked God why you experienced a failure? If so, what did He say? If not, why?

Pursue Change

This week, address any failure that has happened in your life with the only One who has the answers.

1. Ask God what happened.
2. Pinpoint the short circuit. Know who, what, why, when, where, and how so it doesn't happen again.
3. Ask God how to fix it.
4. Get the plan on how to restore any loss.
5. Work the plan and move forward.

Notes

Week 11

Find Your Answers in the Kingdom

completed in all their vast array. By the seventh day God had finished the work he had been doing; so on the seventh day he rested from all his work. And God blessed the seventh day and made it holy, because on it he rested from all the work of creating that he had done.

—Genesis 2:1-3

"All the answers you need to thrive and stay on assignment, allowing you to discover your purpose, are in the Kingdom."

—*Your Financial Revolution: The Power of Rest*

God did not rest on the seventh day because He was tired. God does not get tired. He rested because, as the text says, everything was complete and He was finished. He created man at the end of the sixth day of creation to live in the seventh day. The seventh day had no thought of fear, survival thinking, sickness, and no painful labor or sweat to obtain provision. Instead, Adam's thoughts would only be on God, his wife, his assignment, and purpose. Everything he needed to support his assignment and life were prepared and available; God's plan was complete. People today dream of having what Adam had, an existence free from care, having the ability to focus on their passions and relationships with no concern about provision. Unfortunately, when Adam rebelled, he lost God's provision, and man has been forced to run (painful toil and sweat) after the things of life ever since.

> *For the pagans run after all these things, and your heavenly Father knows that you need them. But seek first his kingdom and his righteousness, and all these things will be given to you as well.*
> —Matthew 6:32-33

The weight of finding provision is a heavy burden and warps man's perception of life. The lure of wealth, to be free from the painful toil and sweat demands of survival, is what people dream about. Being a millionaire only has meaning by its supposed ability to alleviate the stress and weight of finding provision, allowing us to focus on purpose

Week 11: Find Your Answers in the Kingdom

and assignment. The lottery is extremely popular because it offers provision with no labor attached and an escape from the earth curse financial system. Get-rich-quick schemes abound in every form and continually bombard our emails and Facebook posts.

So in the context of our finances, we need to answer a question: Is there a way to go back to that seventh day where everything is complete and intact and available? The answer is a big YES! How that happens and understanding the laws of the Kingdom that will produce that kind of result is the purpose of this book. I know your experience with life or even the church and Christians may argue that what I am saying cannot be true, as so many Christians have embraced the "poverty is holy" theology. But I assure you all the answers you need to thrive and stay on assignment, allowing you to discover your purpose, are in the Kingdom.

Today, as a pastor, I find that the biggest question people ask me is, "What am I supposed to do with my life?" The reason they ask is because in the earth realm since Adam, the quest for provision is the goal by which everything else is measured. Decisions are usually made on the basis of money and not purpose. Money and the need for it can force people to take jobs they hate. In reality, most people do not have a clue who they really are. Mark this down, "Until you know God, you will never know His design for your life. He is the One who created you."

People are so hungry to find out who they are. In the world they seem to be just a number, but to God, they are a very special and unique creation with skills and potential that no one else has. But because they do not know God and, thus, do not know themselves, they look for their value in all the wrong places. They allow the culture to dictate their value by accepting what the culture says. But the image the media portrays and the mirror of the culture are all shifting shadows. By the time you think you are stepping in line with what it calls acceptable, you will find that it has changed and you are already behind.

—*Your Financial Revolution: The Power of Rest*

Prayer Focus

Thank God for giving you access to the knowledge of the secrets of the Kingdom of heaven (Matthew 13:11). Ask Him to show you the answers you need and to direct your path.

Week 11: Find Your Answers in the Kingdom

Think on It

> What would your life be like if you knew exactly where you should go and what you should do in order to be successful?

> How would things be different for you if you knew what your next step should be?

> Do you believe God cares about the small things in your life as well as the big things?

Pursue Change

This week, meditate on Proverbs 3:5-6 (NKJV): *"Trust in the Lord with all your heart, and lean not on your own understanding; in all your ways acknowledge Him, and He shall direct your paths."*

Trust God with your problems and with your questions. Work on actively listening to what God has to say in order to walk out His great plan for your life.

Notes

Notes

Week 12
Decide What Success Is to You

synagogues that Jesus is the Son of God. All those who heard him were astonished and asked, "Isn't he the man who raised havoc in Jerusalem among those who call on this name? And hasn't he come here to take them as prisoners to the chief priests?"

—Acts 9:20-21

"Success is not what you have or who others say you are—success is who God says you are."

—*Better Than You Think*

Let's take a look at the apostle Paul. In a lot of ways, his life was not a picture of success. At least not the "sports car, large house" model of success many honor today. But if we look at Paul's life in the light that over 2,000 years later we are still talking about his life and his legacy, he was one of the most successful men that ever lived.

Paul started off under the name of Saul. He murdered Christians for a living in the early church as a zealous Jewish Pharisee. That was his full-time job! I believe most people wrote Saul off as too far gone for God. People probably thought God wanted Saul dead! His past was too marred, too dysfunctional, and too sinful for him to change his ways and become a "Christ-follower"! He made some really big mistakes.

After Saul came to know Christ, his transformation was so radical that his former peers were enraged with jealousy and called for his death.

Even though many people discounted Saul as damaged goods, judged him, and even tried to kill him, God saw the potential for success in Saul, just like He sees the potential for success in you.

Saul was given the name of Paul after his conversion, and he began to profoundly change the world for God.

Paul wrote 13 books in the New Testament. He wrote more

Week 12: Decide What Success Is to You

of the New Testament than any other one author. Talk about God's restoration! Talk about a success story!

There is no such thing as a hopeless situation with God. People may misjudge you, discount your ability or value, or wrong you—but God sees your potential for success, and He never gives up on you.

Paul went from being a "successful" lawman who killed Christians to a Christian being hunted by lawmen. Still, even when life was miles away from the picture of success, Paul constantly sounded a declaration of joy and victory. He said, "*We can rejoice, too, when we run into problems and trials, for we know that they help us develop endurance*" (Romans 5:3, NLT). Paul gave up temporary status and prestige for a life dedicated to Christ. And, in turn, he found success and joy greater than money or fame could offer him.

When you get your priorities right with God and when you are living successfully according to God's standard, then that produces a joy in your life that nothing else can beat. If you can't be happy with where you are now, then you won't be happy with where you will be tomorrow. You can only be as successful as your attitude. If you are depending on your success or people's opinions to give you happiness, you will be on an emotional roller coaster. Trust me, I've been there.

Success is not what you have or who others say you are—success is who God says you are. God wants to bless you and give you nice things, but without an understanding of God's perfect love and plan for your life, those things will never satisfy you.

You have to decide what success is to you, both in a spiritual and physical form. When you put goals and reminders in front of you, you can live deliberately. Whether it is getting out of debt or leading 10 people to Christ, it is important to have milestones by which to track your progress.

Take a moment and try this: Define your personal success in three very specific points. Write them down, and put them somewhere where you will see them daily—on your bathroom mirror or on your refrigerator door. Start renewing your mind to the picture of success in your life.

Success isn't going to catch you by surprise. It's an intention. It's a decision. It's a mindset. Be prayerful as you go forward, and be aware of what God is speaking to you. Choose to walk this process out with focus and determination. Your life was designed to be a decision, not a reaction. You deserve the life you tolerate, so fight for good things in your life!

—Better Than You Think

Week 12: Decide What Success Is to You

Prayer Focus

Thank God for having a system in place to change you, mature you, and to train you, even if it's uncomfortable. Tell Him how excited you are to go to the next level with His help.

Think on It

→ What does success look like to you?

→ Has your definition of success changed over time? If so, how? If not, why?

→ If your success was being measured by your attitude, how successful would you be right now?

Pursue Change

This week, do exactly what the *Better Than You Think* excerpt instructed: Take a moment and define your personal success in three very specific points. Write them down, and put them somewhere where you will see them daily—on your bathroom mirror or on your refrigerator door. Start renewing your mind to the picture of success in your life.

Notes

Notes

Week 13

Believe That You Have Received

"Just like the wind cannot be seen but has a visible effect on the natural realm, so the Kingdom of God is real and has an effect in the natural realm."

—*Your Financial Revolution: The Power of Allegiance*

When I first met Don, he had come to my office very discouraged and in debt. Nothing seemed to be going right in his life at the time.

Despite all the things going against Don, I saw potential in him. He was willing to learn and willing to work. That powerful combination intrigued me enough to hire him and invest myself in the welfare of his future. In the end, it was an investment that paid huge dividends for both of us.

My fledgling company had just won a trip to Hawaii from one of our vendors, and I felt this would be a great chance to share with Don about the Kingdom of God. Although Don was a Christian, he didn't have the same understanding I did. And although I'd tried on several occasions to share God's principles with him in this area, he just didn't seem to believe what I was saying.

I kept looking for a way to catch Don's attention that would help him realize that he, too, could have success by learning how God's Kingdom worked. However, Don was so discouraged that he had a hard time believing in himself and believing that change could really happen. I knew this Hawaii trip was my chance.

In the weeks before Don and I were to leave, we talked of what we would see and do there. One special interest held Don's attention like no other. He wanted to catch a blue marlin in the beautiful waters of the Pacific Ocean.

Week 13: Believe That You Have Received

"Hawaii is the blue marlin capital of the world," Don told me excitedly. "I've always wanted to catch a blue marlin; it's been a dream of mine." For the first time in weeks, I saw a gleam in Don's eyes. Something actually got him excited, and I knew his excitement would open the door to a powerful lesson.

"Don," I said, "did you know that it is possible to *know*, not hope, but *know* that you will catch a blue marlin in Hawaii by tapping into the Kingdom of God?" I took some time to help him understand the Kingdom and how to release his faith. And so, before we left on our trip, he and his wife sowed, prayed in agreement, and believed that he had received a blue marlin.

In the meantime, Don did everything he knew to do to uphold his part of the harvest. He did some research on available boats and prices and finally booked with a captain that he felt good about. Everything was set, and we were all so excited about going to the blue waters of Hawaii.

Sail day arrived, and as we boarded the boat, we excitedly told the captain that today was the day we were going to catch a blue marlin. While he expected us to have a successful day fishing for other sport fish, he assured us the odds were not in our favor for catching a blue marlin that day. With two boats on chartered tours every day for the last four months, his crews had only brought in one blue marlin.

After six hours of trolling, we hadn't had a single bite, and I was getting a bit worried that the lack of action might weaken Don's faith. In my concern, I yelled out a question to him. "Don," I yelled from my perch on the bridge above him, "let me ask you a question. When did you receive that blue marlin, when it shows up or when we prayed?"

In confidence, Don strongly replied, "Gary, that's simple. I received it when I prayed." I was excited and confident when I heard his reply. It was then that I knew Don had taken my instruction seriously, and he was determined to have that marlin.

Minutes later, Don's reel began to sing as it bent seaward and the mates yelled, "Fish on!" Don and I weren't surprised as he reeled in that big, beautiful blue marlin, but everyone else on the boat was stunned.

The picture of Don and his fish remains in my office to this day as a testimony to others and a constant reminder to me of the reality of the Kingdom. If the Kingdom worked for the marlin, it would certainly work for everything else he needed in life. For Don, it was just the beginning of realizing the impact the Kingdom of God could have on his life.

—Your Financial Revolution: The Power of Allegiance

Week 13: Believe That You Have Received

Prayer Focus

Ask God to show you a glimpse of the great story He has for your life. Thank Him for all He is doing in your life.

Think on It

→ What do people see about God when they look at your life?

→ Are you demonstrating God's love and His Kingdom to a world that is watching you? If so, how? If not, why?

What does the following statement mean to you?

→ As far as God is concerned, whatever you might be dealing with is a legal matter that was already settled 2,000 years ago in a spiritual court of law.

Pursue Change

This week, read Hebrews 11, or what we like to call "The Faith Hall of Fame." It lists all the people in the Bible who acted in faith and changed their world as a result. When you study this chapter, you recognize that there are certain traits that all people of faith exhibit.

Notes

Notes

Week 14
Have the Right Response

Week 14: Have the Right Response

But the fruit of the Spirit is love, joy, peace, forbearance, kindness, goodness, faithfulness, gentleness and self-control. Against such things there is no law.

—Galatians 5:22-23

"All too often, we want to force others to think or believe what we want, but without presenting ourselves in a positive aspect, whether it's a business proposition or the life-changing Gospel, negativity can spoil the possibility of a great outcome."

—*Better Than You Feel*

Every single attribute of the fruit of the Spirit is positive and essential to our character. Patience and long-suffering can be the holding forces to see our vision through until completion. Without them, we can give in quickly to negative circumstances when all we really needed was to have more staying power to fight the good fight to victory. Self-control helps us harness our feelings so that they don't run roughshod over relationships with outbursts of anger and fits of rage or, even more subtly but deadly, with sharp, critical words. Self-control gives us the power to hold our tongues until a better time to speak with more composure and thoughtfulness. Where there are many words, there is much sin (Proverbs 10:19).

If you are a person of many words, ask God to help you use those words in a way to honor and inspire others. When angry, pray first and allow the Holy Spirit to help you with the best use of your words. Then find an acceptable way to process and break down the situation into some form of positive action. Lastly, look for the right timing to address the situation.

Pray → Process → Positive Action → Timing

Every manifestation of the fruit of the Spirit is the working of love. How do we cultivate love? By cultivating the fruit of love. That's what love looks like. Love is kind—kindness. It's patient—patience. It displays goodness, faithfulness, and self-control. When we allow these to garner and work

Week 14: Have the Right Response

in our lives, they bring peace and joy, giving our lives true freedom. To be held captive by negative thoughts and actions is to be controlled not by the Spirit but, rather, by others and their actions, and oftentimes by oppressive spirits like the spirits working in the women at my speaking invitation.

In contrast to the nine fruits of the Spirit, there are hundreds of emotions we could label as "negative." But in a way, emotions are emotions. They really aren't negative, but rather, they are neutral in the sense that they are reactions to something we experience. The actions we take determine their negativity or positivity. If I feel fear, there is probably some sort of danger or perceived concern. How do I respond to that danger? If it is a real threat that I am responding to, my "feelings" or emotions could give me the indicator I need to react. We must analyze the situation to determine whether there is a real danger or whether we are responding to a perception from preprogrammed experiences or past hurts. Processing the right reaction to the perceived danger determines whether I succeed or not in handling the situation.

For instance, I can feel a sense of fear as the roller coaster begins to climb the first and longest hill, anticipating the fast and furious decline. But in the process of evaluating the situation, I analyze the danger along with the fact that the roller coaster is designed to handle the hill safely. Now, I can turn my fear into excitement and, eventually, the gratification of tackling that hill. I might even put my hands up next time because I faced the fear and conquered it. On the other hand, if there is a tiger on my back porch and I stumble upon it, my response may be different!

The real key to turning every emotional response or feeling into positive action is analyzing the apparent situation from God's perspective instead of just your own. Regardless of the circumstance, God has a higher perspective of the problem or conflict. I'm not just speaking metaphorically either! He has an answer to the situation and the proper response, and He can lead you and give you the power to act as He guides you through the turmoil.

I am reminded of a situation where an angry mob sought to destroy Jesus, but the Bible says that God caused Him to slip through the crowd (John 10). God can give you His ability to walk through a difficult situation by letting Him show you the proper response and even divine strategy, whether it may be a relationship breakdown, a hostile crowd, an empty bank account, or a doctor's negative report. God has a positive course of action to get you to your destination.

—Better Than You Feel

Week 14: Have the Right Response

Prayer Focus

Thank God that the fruit of the Spirit is obvious in your life. Ask Him to help you use your words in a way to honor and inspire others.

Think on It

→ What attribute of the fruit of the Spirit would you consider to be your biggest strength? Why?

→ What attribute of the fruit of the Spirit would you consider to be your biggest weakness? Why?

→ Do you have an example of a time that God helped you walk through a difficult situation by giving you the proper response or a divine strategy?

Pursue Change

This week, pray and think about what you've been holding onto that you need to surrender to God. What's been stopping you? Make this the week that you release it.

Notes

Notes

Week 15
Get the Instruction You Need

"Now, I believe this is a controversial topic in many churches—not because it's not in the Bible but because the devil hates it so much."

—*Your Financial Revolution: The Power of Strategy*

You would have to agree that there are many times when you need instruction to know which way to go, to understand a situation, or to make the right decision. This is what praying in tongues can help you with: to edify you or to bring instruction to your life.

Paul tells us that we have a problem and a weakness: "*We do not know what to pray for.*" You may ask, "Why is this a weakness?" We can understand why this is a weakness by reading 1 John 5:14-15.

> *This is the confidence we have in approaching God; that if we ask anything according to his will, he hears us. And if we know that he hears us—whatever we ask—we know we have what we asked of him.*

Without knowing or being confident of the will of God, we cannot operate in faith (being in agreement with God); and if we cannot operate in faith, then we are surely in a weak state because we will not be able to tap into the grace or the power of God without faith being present. So Paul says that not knowing how to pray is a weak condition that praying in tongues can help.

Our weakness is that we don't know how to pray! The Bible doesn't tell us who to marry, where to live, or what job to take. Without knowing the will of God, we can't know and believe that we receive from God when we pray. Again, this is a huge weakness! We have no confidence in God when

Week 15: Get the Instruction You Need

we don't know what His will is. But there is a way that we can discern the will of God in every situation in life. There's a way that we can be sure of God's will so we can operate in faith and in confidence.

That's what Paul is talking about. This edification he is talking about means having access to this kind of knowledge—the knowledge that comes by the Spirit of God. And we tap into hearing the Spirit by praying in the Spirit, or in tongues.

We are not limited to simple human judgment, but we can make judgments about all things with God's help. This is great news! We have the ability, by praying in the Spirit (tongues), to receive mysteries, things we did not know; and by that knowledge, we are able to make right judgments or decisions about all things!

The Baptism of the Holy Spirit is God's secret weapon! He can download His will into the earth without the devil knowing what is going on. In fact, praying in the Spirit is listed as part of our spiritual armor in Ephesians 6:18a:

> *And pray in the spirit on all occasions with all kinds of prayers and requests.*

Praying in the Spirit allows us to pick up on strategies that will allow us to sidestep the enemy, or to advance with unique and unusual tactics.

The implied benefit is that we can make right decisions in life by tapping into the mind of Christ. I think you would have to agree that this is vital! I have found it to be so!

As an example, I can remember having to make a huge decision in regard to my business. So I prayed in the Spirit for a couple of days. But I still could not hear the answer that I needed.

Drenda and I often take our kids to a great amusement park that is a couple of hours away called Cedar Point. It is actually the biggest roller coaster park in the United States, and we usually go there a couple of times a year. It was a Friday night, and I had to have the answer on Monday morning as to what to do. I decided that it would be good to just get my mind on something else for a bit and decided to take Drenda up to the amusement park for the evening. As I was standing in line, not even thinking about that decision I had to make by Monday morning, all of a sudden, I knew exactly what to do. It was as clear as day.

So here is a major key to success—pray! And pray in the Spirit often so that all will go well with you and you will make right decisions, as well as pick up on the mysteries of strategy that you need to win.

—Your Financial Revolution: The Power of Strategy

Week 15: Get the Instruction You Need

Prayer Focus

Thank God for His heart to bring restoration back to the earth and for giving you His Spirit to guide you! Ask Him to help you be a witness for Him on the earth.

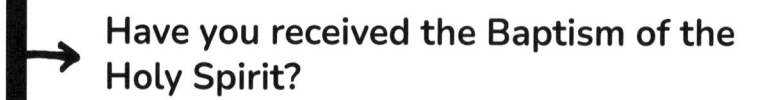

Think on It

→ Have you received the Baptism of the Holy Spirit?

→ Have you tapped into the power of the Holy Spirit in your life?

→ Why do you think the Baptism of the Holy Spirit is so controversial in churches?

Pursue Change

This week, meditate on the following Scriptures and consider whether or not you've been allowing God to use you. Have you been bringing God on the scene, using the power He has given you, or letting it go to waste?

The Spirit of the Sovereign Lord is on me, because the Lord has anointed me to preach good news to the poor. He has sent me to bind up the brokenhearted, to proclaim freedom for the captives and release from darkness for the prisoners, to proclaim the year of the Lord's favor and the day of vengeance of our God, to comfort all who mourn.
—Isaiah 61:1-2

Notes

_____

_____

_____

_____

_____

_____

Notes

Week 16
Break the Curse

will be opened to you. For everyone who asks receives; the one who seeks finds; and to the one who knocks, the door will be opened.

—**Matthew 7:7-8**

"Our mindsets influence the way we filter other people's words and actions. If a conflict has arisen, step back and examine your filter."

—*Nasty Gets Us Nowhere*

Jesus taught us, *"Seek and you will find"* (Matthew 7:7). This spiritual principle applies to everything in our lives, both good and bad.

When we believe something, we have a tendency to make it happen. If we believe men are the problem, then we will find supporting evidence to prove it. If we believe women are impossible to please, then we will be able to cite circumstances to back that up. If we believe marriage is a pain and divorce is inevitable, that will most likely become our experience.

Our mindsets influence the way we filter other people's words and actions. If a conflict has arisen, step back and examine your filter. Is a preconceived mindset affecting your ability to read the situation?

Obviously, with every endeavor, there are challenges and investments that must be made. However, we can't look at the cost alone without also recognizing the benefits and rewards or we will reject the idea altogether. That's the danger of the anti-marriage, pro-women/anti-men, or anti-women messaging of today. If we hear it long enough—which isn't hard to do thanks to daily media propaganda and messaging—we believe it. We buy into the remediation, creating false beliefs about the possibility of working and succeeding together or experiencing lasting relational commitment.

Week 16: Break the Curse

Without commitment, the benefits and joys of relationship with the opposite sex will fail. It was doomed to begin with because of wrong beliefs that the effort and risk weren't worth the return or benefit. That sly serpent Satan has been brainwashing the world ever since he first said, *"Did God really say…?"* (See Genesis 3:1.) We are witnessing a great delusion of lies and challenges against God's good plans for women and men.

So can we get along without getting nasty? This is the golden question!

Probably not, if you're trying to turn him or her into a dog that graduated from obedience school, or expect them to provide you with lifelong bliss. First, dogs are pets—and people are not pets. Second, there is no instant gratification in relationships, no quick fix or euphoric bliss every day. People don't do what you want all the time (neither do pets), but relationships done well, seasoned with age and maturity, satisfy the soul and offer companionship that is beyond any other, certainly more than any pet, bottle of wine, or slice of cheesecake.

Jesus told the woman at the well that He could give her a drink and she would never thirst again. For women and men to first get along, we must drink from this well of life-giving love. We can't give each other something we do not possess.

Only by breaking the curse can we find wholeness and happiness. Years of working in business and ministry, and building a fulfilling marriage, have taught me practical, spiritual principles that will help men and women communicate better, understand each other better, work together, and, most importantly, honor one another.

We *can* break the curse off our relationships and truly succeed together. That was God's plan in the beginning, and it's still His plan for us today.

God loves women and men. He created marriage as a beautiful union between them, and He sent His Son, Jesus, to break the curses that have plagued men and women, to restore His original vision for the relationship between them. Men and women both have a voice in the world, and we need to figure out how to shift our relationships to affirm what God says and how He says our relationships will work. We must shift from the darkness of the curse into the light of God's Kingdom of hope and faith in one another.

—Nasty Gets Us Nowhere

Week 16: Break the Curse

Prayer Focus

Ask God to help you see the positive, the benefits, and the joys, and to overlook the negatives in all of your relationships.

Think on It

→ In what ways do you recognize the enemy has tried to harden your heart in your marriage or other relationships?

→ What are some things you know you can do to strengthen your marriage or other relationships?

→ What do you think your spouse, child, friend, and coworker would say if you asked them how you could better support them? (Consider actually asking!)

Pursue Change

This week, challenge yourself to live selflessly. Give up control. Love on others. When you recognize areas where you know you are usually selfish, admit it and ask God for help to live more like Jesus.

Notes

Notes

Week 17
Know Your Legal Rights

For no matter how many promises God has made, they are "Yes" in Christ. And so through him the "Amen" is spoken by us to the glory of God.

—2 Corinthians 1:20

"There are over 7,000 promises in the Bible that define your legal rights as a child of God."

—*Your Financial Revolution: The Power of Provision*

Let's say that I gave you a $1,000 check. You would thank me, and in your mind, you would have $1,000. You would act like you had $1,000, talk like you had $1,000, and again thank me for the $1,000. But the fact of the matter is you would not have $1,000; you would have a promissory note. The check would simply be a promise that I gave you stating that you had a legal right to receive $1,000 from my bank. You would still have to cash the check to actually have the money! But since my intent toward you was known, as I willingly gave you the check and I signed it, and because you trusted that I had the $1,000, you would say you had $1,000 when all you really had was a promise.

God is certainly greater than I am. His Word does not lie. He gives us His great and precious promises. If God gives you His promise, it is as good as done! The only thing Satan can do to stop the promise from coming to pass is to make you suspicious of God's Word. This is why it is vital that you know that God is good and does not lie.

Let me give you another example. I know many have heard that miracles have passed away and God does not do the same things that Jesus did as He walked on the earth. I grew up in a very traditional church, and I never saw the power of God manifested. So just because I did not see people getting healed, does that mean that God does not heal any longer? To answer that, we cannot go by our experiences. We need to find out what the Bible says, what the King's law says about healing.

Week 17: Know Your Legal Rights

> *How God anointed Jesus of Nazareth with the Holy Spirit and power, and how he went around doing good and healing all who were under the power of the devil, because God was with him.*
> —Acts 10:38

As we can see, healing was a key signature of Jesus's ministry. The text says that Jesus healed all because God was with Him. Now that phrase, "*God was with him*" is a statement that you need to understand. Of course, God was with Jesus His entire life on the earth. But this phrase is actually referring to the moment when Jesus was being water baptized and the Holy Spirit descended on Him like a dove. God was with Him doing the work.

Well, you might say, "Yes, Jesus healed, but He is not here." Well I agree, you are correct, but He passed that assignment on to the church. You see, that same power that came on Jesus was also given to the church. As Jesus is about to leave the earth, He tells His disciples the following.

> *But you will receive power when the Holy Spirit comes on you; and you will be my witnesses in Jerusalem, and in all Judea and Samaria, and to the ends of the earth.*
> —Acts 1:8

This same power, the Holy Spirit, came upon the church to do the same miracles that Jesus did.

You cannot tell me anything different. My own daughter Amy had a 13-pound tumor in her abdomen. We all prayed for her healing based on God's Word, and she went to bed then woke up in the morning completely healed. The 13-pound tumor was gone, and her back (which was knotted and twisted) was completely reconstructed. You can see and read her story in her book *Healed Overnight*.

My daughter-in-law had a tumor the size of an orange on her side, which the doctors said would have to be removed by surgery. They said she had a rare form of cancer and had one to two months to live. She also believed the promises of God and woke up in the morning completely healed. The tumor was gone.

Drenda also had a huge growth the size of a 50-cent piece on her back. She began to command it to leave her body, and within two weeks, it was completely gone as well.

Did God choose to heal these ladies? Did He like these three ladies better than you? No! They understood the laws and benefits of the Kingdom and simply laid claim to them.

—Your Financial Revolution: The Power of Provision

Week 17: Know Your Legal Rights

Prayer Focus

Thank God that His promise of healing IS evident in your life.

Think on It

→ Can you confidently say that you believe Jesus already paid for your healing? Why or why not?

→ Do you have a hard time seeing past the symptoms in order to walk out your faith?

→ In what area of your life do you most need healing (mentally, physically, financially, etc.)?

Pursue Change

This week, determine that you are going to stand on the promise of healing. When the symptoms speak loudly, slam the door and walk away. Don't allow the enemy to discourage you when you're standing on the promises of God because of what you feel. Focus on what the Kingdom of God says. Stop looking at the symptoms, and look at examples of healing—of deliverance. Change the picture you see.

Notes

Notes

Week 18

Build on the Rock

Week 18: Build on the Rock

There is a way that appears to be right, but in the end it leads to death.

— Proverbs 14:12

"The enemy is looking for an open door in all of our lives. Getting our feelings hurt and harboring an offense over it is the number one way I know he enters lives—next to blatant disobedience or rebellion."

—*Shark Proof*

If we live in a place of hurt, how can we be effective in our own lives or in impacting others? Hurt feelings destroy so many relationships. Not only that, but they can take us off course from our destinies if we let them. We all do and say things that unintentionally hurt people at times. Most of these slights and misunderstandings are just that—misunderstandings! No matter what others do to us, we have to make the choice to walk in integrity, forgiveness, and to stay the course. You can't build a strong house on a crooked foundation.

> *Therefore everyone who hears these words of mine and puts them into practice is like a wise man who built his house on the rock. The rain came down, the streams rose, and the winds blew and beat against that house; yet it did not fall, because it had its foundation on the rock. But everyone who hears these words of mine and does not put them into practice is like a foolish man who built his house on sand. The rain came down, the streams rose, and the winds blew and beat against that house, and it fell with a great crash.*
> —Matthew 7:24-27

Don't build your life on a sandbar!

It's sad to see how mean-spirited and intolerant people can be while demanding tolerance for "their" views. While we can't change this in others, we can work on our relationships and especially ourselves.

Week 18: Build on the Rock

After years of working with people and observing my own shortcomings, I've come to the conclusion that our egos, or may I say our pride, often gets in the way of relationships. We're all looking for others to make us feel special, valued, and even exceptional; and when others fail to do what we need, we get our feelings hurt. We retreat, sulk, and even punish the other person with our withdrawal! I've watched friendships be destroyed, marriages broken, families devastated, businesses fail, and, worse, God's Kingdom hindered, all because of pride.

Social media has created an opportunity for people to take their hurts to a whole new level of name-calling. For a generation that has been indoctrinated with tolerance messaging, when their toes get stepped on, they are the most intolerant versions of themselves. It's that type of pride that makes us expect the other person to fix things while neglecting any personal responsibility. Of course, that's the message being pushed in this hour, to live for the moment and do what feels good instead of what is right because it's right.

The culture is out of control, and we can't afford to fall into their divisive worldly attitudes, which lead to rebellious ways. If we follow celebrity culture, we will end up with their results—an over 80 percent divorce rate and the highest incidences of drug/alcohol abuse and early deaths/suicides in the culture. And these are our role models? I don't think so! Yet they are fueling the division they scream against. There are times we disagree with others, but we must disagree with respect.

That's the confusion of the hour. In the last days, people will be lovers of self, lovers of pleasure, lovers of money, abusive, slanderers, disobedient to parents, boastful, and proud. Have you noticed any of this in today's culture? To stay true to God's purpose for our lives, we must divorce celebrity values and realign our beliefs and actions with something higher than paid actors.

I've been married 36 years, have raised a successful family, and experienced solid financial freedom while all along the way struggling to swim upstream—with the culture quick to mow my family down if allowed. Gary and I continue to experience a good life because we didn't take the short route to success through compromise. We were tempted at times, and, yes, there was a price to go against the grain, but I'm grateful we did! Sure, we've made some mistakes along the way, but God has a way of helping us all course correct when we submit our attitudes and humble ourselves before His Word and ways.

Recently, a minister said on social media, "We don't need more truth tellers." I couldn't disagree more. We do need to tell the truth (with love.) It is the truth that sets people free.

Jesus is not a way to truth; He is THE way.

—Shark Proof

Week 18: Build on the Rock

Prayer Focus

Thank God for Jesus—the way, the truth, and the life—and the powerful work He has done and is continuing to do in you.

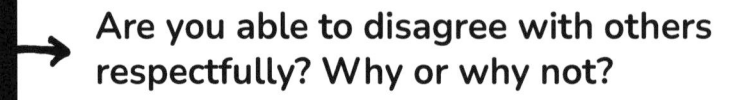

Think on It

→ Are you able to disagree with others respectfully? Why or why not?

→ Has your pride ever gotten in the way of a relationship? How?

→ Are you able to confidently share the Truth of Jesus? Why or why not?

Pursue Change

This week, pray fervently for our culture, our world, and our governments. Government has the power to affect your life more than anything else in the earth realm. The culture and the enemy want to keep believers from getting involved. Do the opposite. But don't just spew opinions on social media.

Start with prayer, and actually get involved. There is a battle, and we MUST fight for the standards set for us by the Word of God. Know the facts and speak up. Take a stand. Vote. Embrace and honor the Word of God. Teach your children to stand for truth, righteousness, and honor. Be willing to intercede and fight the good fight.

Notes

Notes

Week 19
Fund God's Assignments

One person gives freely, yet gains even more; another withholds unduly, but comes to poverty.

—Proverbs 11:24

"God always funds His assignments—always!"

—*Your Financial Revolution: The Power of Generosity*

Let me set the stage of what happened in 1 Kings 17. There is a severe drought going on, and the brook where Elijah is staying is drying up. He must now move to a new location to find food and water. God speaks to him and directs him to *"Go at once to Zarephath in the region of Sidon and stay there. I have directed a widow there to supply you with food."* It should be noted that Zarephath was a Canaanite town and was not part of the nation of Israel at the time.

As Elijah approaches the city, he sees a widow gathering sticks, and he calls out to her to give him some water. *"As she was going to get it, he called, 'And bring me, please, a piece of bread.'"* She answers that she is basically out of food as there is only enough for one more meal for her son and herself.

But then the prophet does something extremely strange, something that you may even feel is unthinkable considering the circumstances. He tells her to go home and make him a loaf and actually bring it to him before she makes one for her own family. Understanding how that may sound, he prefaces the instructions with the words, *"Don't be afraid."* Then he declares to her the following:

> *For this is what the Lord, the God of Israel, says: "The jar of flour will not be used up and the jug of oil will not run dry until the day the Lord sends rain on the land."*
>
> —1 Kings 17:14

Week 19: Fund God's Assignments

Wow, what will she do? Will she believe him and give him her son's last meal?

> *She went away and did as Elijah had told her. So, there was food every day for Elijah and for the woman and her family. For the jar of flour was not used up and the jug of oil did not run dry, in keeping with the word of the Lord spoken by Elijah.*
> —1 Kings 17:15-16

She did believe him, and pay close attention to the result—there was food every day for Elijah and for the woman and her family. Let me change one word and say that again: There was food every day for God's assignment and food for the woman and her family.

So, let me ask you a question: "Did it cost the widow anything to give that last meal away?" No, it did not. It saved her life.

Why did the prophet insist that she make his cake first? Not with hers but separate. He even asked that she bring it to him before she started baking her own. (Remember, you want to be a spiritual scientist and ask questions.)

The prophet knew that when she gave him (God's assignment) the first cake, her oil and flour changed kingdoms. They then came under the jurisdiction of the Kingdom of God. It was only then that God could legally make the flour and oil multiply.

God had Elijah on assignment. He needed provision to carry out His assignment. We know that Elijah was a prophet, so he carried the Word of the Lord wherever God would send him. But God needed His assignment funded, and that always involves people.

Since there was no one in Israel who had the faith to believe Him, God had to go outside of Israel to another nation where He found a widow who had a heart of faith. And as we said earlier, Elijah was sent to this specific widow because God knew she would believe Him.

By putting God first and obeying the word of the Lord to her, God's assignment, Elijah, was taken care of, as well as her family, throughout the entire famine.

When God has things to get done, He looks over the earth to find someone that He can trust, someone who will obey Him and carry out His plans. He also needs people who will finance His agenda.

If you want to have big ideas, if you want God to download great business concepts to you, you have to qualify for them! God knows your heart, and He is looking over the earth for those He can trust with His assignments. He is looking to see who He can trust to fund His assignments. He will then send that person the plan He has for gathering the money that is needed. Do you see it?

Week 19: Fund God's Assignments

God looks for those who have hearts of obedience to fund His assignments!

—Your Financial Revolution: The Power of Generosity

Prayer Focus

Ask God to help you have a heart of obedience to help fund His assignments as well as to carry them out. Thank Him for giving you the provision to carry out His assignments.

Think on It

→ Have you ever felt God leading you to do something, but you didn't know where the money was going to come from? What happened?

→ Do you believe God can trust you with His assignments? Why or why not?

→ Do you believe God can trust you to fund His assignments? Why or why not?

Pursue Change

This week, meditate on 2 Corinthians 9:6-8:

Remember this: Whoever sows sparingly will also reap sparingly, and whoever sows generously will also reap generously. Each of you should give what you have decided in your heart to give, not reluctantly or under compulsion, for God loves a cheerful giver. And God is able to bless you abundantly, so that in all things at all times, HAVING ALL THAT YOU NEED, you will abound in every good work.

Giving is the doorway that gives God the opening to bless you with opportunities, direction, concepts, and ideas that will propel your life financially. Ask God to show you where He wants you to sow this week.

Notes

_____
_____
_____
_____
_____

Notes

Week 20

Conquer Excuses

happen, it will be done for them."
—**Mark 11:22-23**

"God can't lie. When He says that nothing will be impossible for you, He is promising that nothing will be impossible for you."

—*Better Than You Think*

You are capable of anything.

Matthew 17:20b says, *"Truly I tell you, if you have faith as small as a mustard seed, you can say to this mountain, 'Move from here to there,' and it will move. Nothing will be impossible for you."*

Isn't that encouraging?

I find for a lot of people that verse isn't as thrilling as it should be. It has no power to them. It has no promise to them. I can't believe that! If you believed what that verse really says, you would be jumping up and down. You would toss this book to the side and run around your house laughing and praising God. No joke!

The reason many people don't react when they read that verse is because they don't believe it. They have it on a plaque on their wall, but they don't even know the revelation that verse has to change their lives. God can't lie. When He says that nothing will be impossible for you, He is promising that nothing will be impossible for you. I meet so many people with incredible potential who don't believe that. They can't see all of the amazing things they are capable of or get a vision for their future, because everything is too good for them, too big for them, or too hard for them.

If you try, you can find a million excuses why you can't. How about a reason why you can? Or why you should? In fact,

Week 20: Conquer Excuses

the Bible says that there is no question of "can" and "can't."

> *"What do you mean, 'If I can?'"* Jesus asked. *"Anything is possible if a person believes."*
> —Mark 9:23 (NLT)

> *I can do all this through him who gives me strength.*
> —Philippians 4:13

Your job is not to figure out if you can or can't. Your job is to ask God if you should, and if that's a yes, your job is to say that you will. That's all! Stop letting the question of "Can I?" hold you back and cripple you with doubt.

What is keeping you from writing your success story?

When we were offered a program on television, we immediately began to look at the cost. We began to think about the expense and the amount of work it required. We began to think about people's eyes on us and that we weren't perfect. We didn't even feel worthy to do it, but we had to see instead that God wanted us to do it. Too many times as believers we ask ourselves, "What is it going to cost me? What price am I going to pay?" Before we know it, we've renewed our minds and talked ourselves out of being bold and courageous.

Your excuses and mental boundaries will hold you back from what God has for you. "*But God*, I can't do that. *But*

God, that's impossible. *But God*, it didn't work before." You have to get your *But God* out of the way!

I always love the story of Colonel Sanders. He was 62 years old when he looked at his first retirement check. He said, "This ain't gonna cut it!" He pulled out a fried chicken recipe, started a small restaurant, and the rest is history. He didn't hang up his whole destiny just because he was 62 years old. It is never too late to start doing what God has called you to do.

> *Jesus replied, "What is impossible with man is possible with God."*
> —Luke 18:27

God is on your side. He wants to team up with you and to help you go to the next level. He isn't going to ask you to do something that is not ultimately going to bless you. When you team up with God and trust His Word over your excuses and mental boundaries, your life will transform into an amazing display of His goodness.

> *But seek first his kingdom and his righteousness, and all these things will be given to you as well.*
> —Matthew 6:33

—*Better Than You Think*

Week 20: Conquer Excuses

Prayer Focus

Thank God that He said ALL things are possible with Him. Ask Him to help you overcome any excuses or mental boundaries that are keeping you from the life He has for you.

Think on It

→ When you read Matthew 17:20b, how do you react?

→ Is there a time in your life that you let your excuses stop you from succeeding?

→ What's stopping you right now from writing your success story?

Pursue Change

This is the week to stop tolerating your excuses.

If you start to *think* of excuses for why you can't do something, shut them down and speak Luke 18:27 over your life: *"Jesus replied, "What is impossible with man is possible with God."*

If you start to *speak* out excuses, ask God to forgive you for not walking in power with Him, and go back to this week's Prayer Focus. Then, speak the Word out of your mouth:

> *"What do you mean, 'If I can?'" Jesus asked. "Anything is possible if a person believes."*
> —Mark 9:23 (NLT)

> *I can do all this through him who gives me strength.*
> —Philippians 4:13

Notes

_____

_____

_____

_____

Notes

Week 20
See Yourself as God Does

Week 21: See Yourself as God Does

"For I know the plans I have for you," declares the Lord, "plans to prosper you and not to harm you, plans to give you hope and a future."

—Jeremiah 29:11

"Your perspective needs to change to think like God thinks."

—*Your Financial Revolution: The Power of Rest*

Have you ever heard someone say, "Don't get your hopes up"? Growing up, if I ever was excited about something that my dad thought was foolish, he would say, "Someday you will grow up." Because of that, I usually did not allow myself to dream about anything except what was determined to be needed by my dad. I believe my dad had been hurt by growing up in an alcoholic home, and this is what he had to do while growing up as well.

To be honest, we have all been professional worriers since we were born. Fear is the common vernacular of the earth realm. If you will stop and think about it, the word no has been so ingrained in us from the time we were born. "No, you cannot have that." "No, put that back." "No, you cannot go there." "No, you cannot afford that." Eventually, we just stop saying "Yes" to anything except the occasional escape to an activity that numbs our mind to our actual circumstances, like overeating our favorite comfort food.

One study estimates that the average child hears the words no or don't over 148,000 times while growing up, compared to just a few thousand yes messages.[3]

I recently held our annual Provision Conference, and on the platform I put a 2017 Ferrari, a car to be admired for sure. The owner of the car attends my church and paid cash for the car, which was close to $400,000. As the attendees all

---
[3] "Becoming a Yes Mom," http://www.babyzone.com.

Week 21: See Yourself as God Does

came in, they admired and stared at the car, all looking it over, wanting a closer look. But although they all admired the car, the point I was making by putting it on the platform was not to inspire a lifestyle of material goals but, rather, to teach them a lesson. The people all gathered around the car, all stating they would love to drive it.

I knew the "no" training they had received in the earth curse system of painful toil and sweat was subconsciously shouting, "NO, you will never own a car like that! No, you will never be able to afford that; don't even think about it." Because of the "NO" training they have had, we all have had, most of them there never even considered actually owning a Ferrari because the no mindset could not see it or receive it. However, if I kept changing out cars every hour, from expensive down to the cheapest, eventually, I would have a car up on the platform where they would think and say, "I like that car; I should get one."

What was the difference? It was all about how they saw themselves, their potential, and the cost of the car. Yes, there could have been a few there that said to themselves, "I will own that car someday," or possibly there were people there that had the money and viewed the car differently. But I am sure that for the masses, owning a car like that was not even in their realm of thinking. The millionaire who paid cash for the car actually has a half dozen Ferraris. To his mindset, it is just a great car. When he saw the car, he envisioned owning it and went about the process of ordering it from Italy and then having it shipped to his home in the U.S. It was not hard for him to act on his vision because he had the provision. Here is an important key to rest—provision is pro-vision.

Major Key: Provision Is Pro-vision

Without provision, there is no vision; there is only survival. The earth curse system of poverty has stolen our dreams and our futures. I know the Ferrari was a radical illustration, but it made my point. The people there did not even allow themselves to dream of owning a car like that because they viewed it as unobtainable. If they did even for a moment allow themselves to dream about owning it, their training in the earth curse system would scream back at them, "What a waste of money!" But what if you had $25 billion cash in your checking account (I am just making a point)? That car would seem so cheap that you would buy one just to use it on the weekends.

It is all a matter of perspective, and since the Word of God says every promise of God is "Yes" and "Amen (so be it)," your perspective needs to change to think like God thinks.

—Your Financial Revolution: The Power of Rest

Week 21: See Yourself as God Does

Prayer Focus

Thank God for always helping you look past where you live, what you have, and your present circumstances, and seeing your potential through His eyes. Ask Him to help you dream God-sized dreams.

Think on It

→ How often do you think you say "no" to yourself, to your spouse, to your kids, etc.?

→ Do you believe you think like God thinks?

→ What do you envision for your future?

Pursue Change

You will never possess what you can't SEE.

This week, really envision your future by creating a vision board with words and images of what you're believing for your future.

Not sure what to put on your vision board? Shut out distractions, get alone with God, and listen for His direction. Write down what He reveals to you. Add images that support what He has revealed.

Notes

Notes

Week 22
Think Right Thoughts

"You didn't choose where you were born or how you were raised, and you can't change it. However, you can change what you think, how you act, and how you react to life and people today."

—*Better Than You Feel*

There is a law of the Kingdom of God that says whatever a man (or woman) sows, that they will also reap (Galatians 6:7). This law applies to everything. What we eat, what we think about, what we say. It also has an impact on our emotions and feelings. If I have deficiencies emotionally from what has been sown into my life by others, my environment, upbringing, and myself, those deficiencies will show up in my life. And since we have all been raised in an earth curse system, we all have deficiencies, wounds, and lack from what we've sown and what others have sown into us.

There are many wonderful, natural principles we can learn that will help us deal with our weaknesses and deficiencies. But honestly, without the power of an encounter with God's love and Spirit, those changes and natural methods will fall short of bringing us into a state of wholeness and real lasting freedom. We can learn to accept ourselves and be better communicators, we can forgive others by willpower, but nothing can undo what was done to us or what we have done to others without God. The law of sowing and reaping will keep us in a state of perpetual deficiency. Paul even said, "*I do not understand what I do. For what I want to do I do not do, but what I hate I do*" (Romans 7:15).

I believe in doing everything we can with natural knowledge and wisdom, but it's not enough by itself! We need the Spirit of God to help us supersede natural laws that have created deficiencies in our soul. We need God's power, His spiritual truth coupled with practical principles. God's supernatural

Week 22: Think Right Thoughts

power will give us strength and the ability to do in the natural what we could not do in ourselves. He gives us the ability to change, to sow new thoughts, and to use more powerful Kingdom principles than the natural earthly ways we have learned and lived.

I have seen these principles radically change innumerable people's lives over and over, as well as mine. I have witnessed alcoholics, addicts, and the severely depressed walk free when the natural world and doctors told them there was no hope for their pain and they would only be able to "learn to cope." And while learning to operate in natural ways may be a start in the right direction, complete freedom is much greater and comes only by the supernatural.

All of your thoughts, actions, and reactions originate from your belief system—what you believe about yourself, your worth, and your future.

YOUR BELIEF SYSTEM ORIGINATES FROM:

>YOUR UPBRINGING - "The Past"
>- You didn't choose it.
>- You cannot change it.
>
>YOUR CHOICES - "Today"
>- You can change it by what you "Think."
>- You can change it by how you "Act" and "React."

How are you acting? With confidence and boldness or fear and intimidation? How are you reacting when people mistreat you? When negative circumstances happen in life? Let God's Spirit give you the self-control to manage your life instead of being controlled by the people and circumstances around you.

We have to learn to manage our thoughts and emotions about the past and future—where we've been and where we're going. How can we do that? By managing TODAY!

Where you are going is much more important than where you've been. The pathway to tomorrow is bright if you are looking forward with God toward the future. If you are looking forward, you'll move forward. Your spirit will see vision and dream dreams. You will start to set goals to get to that dream, and strategies will develop that give you the motivation to act on your dream. You are what you think.

Our dreams will not develop into goals and strategies toward accomplishment if we allow emotional baggage from yesterday to distract us or create enough disturbances to discourage us from the decision to act. Facts are clearer, but feelings can become the gray area that stops our progress. The soul (mind, will, and emotions) all must work together in a positive direction, moving forward, for us to have the right mindset, willful decision-making, and emotional responses to energize where we're going. I must think right, decide I will do it, and harness emotions to

Week 22: Think Right Thoughts

succeed. Freedom is a beautiful word, but it can only be attained when the natural and the supernatural collide in a powerful way!

—Better Than You Feel

Prayer Focus

Thank God that He gives you the power to "lay aside every weight and sin and run the race" He has marked for you (Hebrews 12:1).

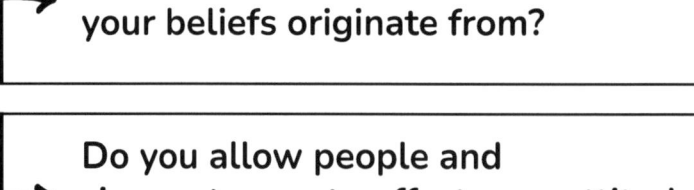

Think on It

→ Have you ever thought about where your beliefs originate from?

→ Do you allow people and circumstances to affect your attitude or control your day?

→ Are you free from carrying emotional baggage?

Pursue Change

This week, use your imagination to picture yourself in a hot air balloon basket waiting for take-off. (Even if you don't care for heights, work with us here.)

You're in this beautiful hot air balloon basket, waiting to leave the ground and soar across the skies, taking in all the breathtaking beauty of God's creation.

But there's a problem. No, not with the balloon—with the sandbags anchoring the balloon to the ground.

See, your mental and emotional baggage—pressures, behaviors, insecurities, and sins—are the sandbags weighing down your hot air balloon. Are there so many sandbags attached to your hot air balloon that you can't leave the ground? Are you stuck?

It's time to lay aside every weight that's holding you back from rising to reach your full potential with God. Fix your eyes on Jesus and let go!

Notes

Week 23

Seek the Kingdom First

So do not worry, saying, "What shall we eat?" or "What shall we drink?" or "What shall we wear?" For the pagans run after all these things, and your heavenly Father knows that you need them. But seek first his kingdom and his righteousness, and all these things will be given to you as well. Therefore do not worry about tomorrow, for tomorrow will worry about itself. Each day has enough trouble of its own.

—Matthew 6:31-34

"You need to throw off that old government of the earth curse system with all of its lack and despair and enjoy a new way of living—living in the Kingdom of God, with new laws, no lack, and great joy!"

—*Your Financial Revolution: The Power of Allegiance*

Jesus says you cannot serve two masters. You may think you can, but you can't. You will love one and only one. I can tell you which one it is. It is the one that you trust to meet your needs. When the Lord spoke to me in that old farmhouse about me never taking the time to learn how His Kingdom worked, He was saying that He was not really my master. He was not the one that I had full confidence in and that I was serving and trusting. Oh, sure, I went to church, was generous, loved God, and knew I was going to heaven. But I had never taken the time to learn God's system of finance and how His Kingdom worked.

> *For where your treasure is, there your heart will be also.*
> —Luke 12:34

God wants to be first in our lives, not money. If money is our treasure, it will be first, demanding our time, our priorities, and affection. This is why Peter was not to leave his assignment to go make money when the tax bill came due. This is why God has to train us to gather and not to labor. Jesus has to teach us the Kingdom way, how to trust God for our provision, thus freeing our hearts to love God with our whole hearts! Jesus said, "*Is not life more than food, and the body more than clothes?*" He was saying that life is not having things. The purpose of life is that those things serve you and your assignment on the earth.

Week 23: Seek the Kingdom First

Yet what do we see? Most people are running nonstop serving those things. People are running to pay the mortgage, to pay the car payment, to pay the bills….

He said in Matthew 6:33 that if you seek first the Kingdom of God and His righteousness, all of these things will be added to your life. The thing is not where we find the problem; it is the heart. If God did not want us to have the things, Jesus would have said so. Instead, He says that all of these things the world runs after shall be added to our lives if we live God's way.

In other words, life is not serving things, but unfortunately, most people are doing just that. They do not have a choice; they are slaves. It is impossible to serve two masters, and serving things is not life. Jesus goes on to explain there is another system, a place of financial peace and provision freeing you to live. It is called the Kingdom.

Jesus gives us two examples of what the Kingdom looks like in His teaching here in Matthew 6. He says, "*Look at the birds of the air; they do not sow or reap or store away in barns, and yet your heavenly Father feeds them*" (v. 26a).

Birds do not have worm farms!

They do not take it upon themselves to provide their daily needs.

No, Father God feeds them. They simply have to gather what they need each day. Do you see it? They do not sweat with painful toil for their very lives. They gather!

> *And why do you worry about clothes? See how the lilies of the field grow. They do not labor or spin. Yet I tell you that not even Solomon in all his splendor was dressed like one of these.*
> —Matthew 6:28-29

The flowers do not dress themselves with painful toil and sweat to make it happen. No, Father dresses them. Jesus goes on and tells you and me our answer. There is another way to live, the Kingdom way! Jesus says, "*Seek first the Kingdom of God and his righteousness, and all these things will be given to you as well*" (Matthew 6:33, EHV). What does "seek the Kingdom of God" mean? It means find out how it works! Study the laws that govern it. Learn how God's system works!

—*Your Financial Revolution: The Power of Allegiance*

Week 23: Seek the Kingdom First

Prayer Focus

Ask God to forgive you for any times that you've run after money or wealth or worried about how you would have provision instead of trusting Him. Ask Him to give you a clear understanding of His Kingdom and how to operate in it.

Think on It

→ Do you actually like your job? Why or why not?

→ If you could make the same amount of money, or more, doing something else, what would it be?

→ Are you running after God or money?

Pursue Change

Take some time this week to really think about whether or not you're seeking God and His Kingdom first or if you're seeking something, or some *things*, first.

Ask God to reveal to you what you might need to change to take the next step toward the destiny He has planned for you.

Notes

Notes

Week 24

Complement Each Other

> *of my flesh; she shall be called "woman," for she was taken out of man.*
>
> —**Genesis 2:23**

> "Men and women have different strengths and weaknesses, but that makes us stronger when we work together!"
>
> —*Nasty Gets Us Nowhere*

When Gary and I were first engaged, he took me dove hunting. Yes, I went from a feminist to trying to impress this man!

Now, for you to truly understand how out of my element I was, you have to know that I was a *city* girl from Georgia. I didn't grow up on a pecan farm or in some sparsely populated town out West. As a young girl, I thought hunting was the grossest, weirdest thing that one could do, and my worst nightmare was marrying a boy from up North who was a hunter. In fact, when I was mad at my parents, I would threaten to marry a Northern boy and move. Ha!

Words have power, because that's exactly what happened. I agreed to go hunting with Gary because it sounded fun and adventurous. I imagined this romantic hunting trip with us two prancing around the woods, like Tarzan and Jane, where I would get a perfect shot, and my fiancé would swoon at having such an incredible future wife… at which point, he would take me shopping.

Gary taught me how to shoot the gun and left me in position. When I saw a flock of birds and I pulled up and shot, Gary came over, laughing a bit at my attempt.

"What?" I asked, my ears still ringing from the gunshot.

"You're cute," he remarked with a coy smile. *Well, that's not quite what I was going for,* I thought, *but I'll take it!*

Week 24: Complement Each Other

It turns out that I shot a bird all right, but it was a sparrow, not a dove. (Yes, I know, His eye is on the sparrow.) Gary hadn't given me any bird species lessons. It never occurred to Mr. Hunter that I didn't know the difference between a dove and a sparrow.

He went on to explain the differences. It was Greek to me. Why did anyone care about the differences? I guess they don't taste the same. Then Gary pulled up, casually shot a dove, and showed me the difference.

Warning: this story is about to get more graphic.

Shockingly, using his thumbs, Gary popped out the bird's breast and stuck it in the pocket of his hunter's jacket.

Gasp! That was the day I decided not to be a hunter but, rather, to be a gatherer—not of birds but of other things… you know, like things I find on sale at the grocery store.

When Gary and I first got married, that was the first time I really realized how different men and women are. Gary and I liked different things, but more importantly, we communicated and saw the world through totally different points of view.

In order for men and women to succeed together, we first have to understand that we *are* different, and we need to understand what *makes* us different. Men and women are not only physiologically very different, but we are also two separate, distinct creations of God. God made man from the dirt and woman from man. We are equal but certainly not the same.

Men and women have different strengths and weaknesses, but that makes us powerful when we work together!

In many ways, we are the same, but in very significant ways, we are not alike at all. It's almost ludicrous that some women have spent their lives fighting to disprove this fact when it doesn't take a rocket scientist to see the undeniable truth. Men or women can try to imitate the other sex, but it's only imitation. Margarine is not butter, no matter what the packaging looks like, nor is burlap silk. Woman was formed from man for companionship with him; God created us to complement each other.

This isn't just proven in the Bible; it's proven in science, too—in human behavior, physiology, biology, and neurology, to name just a few fields. Men and women *are* different. Our DNA and origins tell the story. This is most certainly not an issue of capability or intelligence but of a difference in design. There are general, overarching distinctions between men and women that are universally observed, studied, and recorded in every part of the world. Obviously, each of us is a product of not only God's design but also our environment, experiences, and personal choices. Yet environmental differences do not greatly change the tendencies of human nature and physiological makeup that distinguish us. The

Week 24: Complement Each Other

difference between our genders is a great strength when understood, honored, and utilized, whether in marriage, business, ministry, or culture.

—*Nasty Gets Us Nowhere*

Prayer Focus

Thank God for making men and women different and that those differences make us powerful when we work together. Ask Him to help you understand, honor, and utilize those differences for strength in your marriage, business, or ministry.

Think on It

→ What is one difference you notice between men and women that can be used as a strength when working together?

→ Why do you think the culture is trying to negate God's definition of only man or woman?

→ Are you competing with the opposite gender in your life or complementing them?

Pursue Change

This week, focus on the positive. We all have faults. Sadly, it's human nature to hide our own faults but point out the weaknesses in others. God sees *everyone* as valuable. Try looking at ALL of your relationships the way God does. Find positive things to focus on and things to be grateful for.

Finally, brothers and sisters, whatever is true, whatever is noble, whatever is right, whatever is pure, whatever is lovely, whatever is admirable—if anything is excellent or praiseworthy—think about such things. Whatever you have learned or received or heard from me, or seen in me— put it into practice. And the God of peace will be with you.

—Philippians 4:8-9

Notes

Notes

Week 25

Ask God for the Plan

Thus says the Lord, your Redeemer, The Holy One of Israel: "I am the Lord your God, Who teaches you to profit, Who leads you by the way you should go."

—Isaiah 48:17 (NKJV)

"There is nothing more powerful than having the plan. Without a plan, the picture is a dream, but with a plan, the dream can be built."

—*Your Financial Revolution: The Power of Strategy*

Dan was farming about 1,400 acres in Central Ohio, and it was not going well. In fact, he was not making a profit and was very concerned. But as he kept hearing about the Kingdom and how the Holy Spirit can help, he came to Jennifer one day and said, "I want to double our giving." Jennifer was shocked but so excited. So that is what they did.

That year, their yield on that same 1,400 acres was 128% higher than the year before. It was so much higher, in fact, that they were able to pay cash for a new car and purchase, with cash, another farm, which meant more acreage to plant the following year. Dan was so excited! He said his dad would have taken 10 years to pay off that new farm, and he had just paid cash for it. So I asked Dan how that happened and to tell me the story.

It seemed that after Dan and Jennifer began to double their giving, they would also pray and ask God to show them what to do. Dan says one day as he was going through the normal stack of mail that he usually received each day, most of it marketing ads to farmers, he had just thrown a small three by five card into the trash can when he felt an unction to get it back out. There was nothing special about the little card, another advertisement about a piece of farm equipment. It was inviting farmers to a meeting to discuss the tool.

Dan felt a strange urge to go and, after going to the

Week 25: Ask God for the Plan

meeting, bought the tool that had been advertised. The tool was a new product on the market that aided in planting, something to do with seed placement and soil preparation. Dan tried to explain to me the scientific reasons it was effective in increasing crop yield, but he lost me about halfway through his explanation. But he understood it, and that was what was important. He told me that he was only the second farmer to buy the tool in Ohio at the time. Well, that little tool did the trick, and a 128% increase in yield was the result. Dan went on to acquire more land, and today, he farms thousands of acres. He now has many stories of how the Holy Spirit helped him make decisions that propelled him faster than he ever could have imagined.

So how did Dan change his poor performing farm to one that was making a great profit? He followed his Counselor's, the Holy Spirit's, advice. The sad thing is that most Christians hear that story and have no idea how it happened, which is why I felt it was so important to write this book. No, most Christians will celebrate how great God is, acknowledge that it was a God thing, but have no clue how to duplicate it. We then end up with a bunch of Christians disillusioned with God and blaming God for their troubles. "Where is God? I do not know why God has not helped me" is what I hear a lot of.

I hope you have already realized this by now, but the Kingdom operates by laws, not by favors. God does not pick whom He is going to bless and pick those whom He is not. Dan is not one of God's chosen ones and is not more special to God than you are. You have the same legal rights as Dan does in the Kingdom. Just like anyone has a right to sow seed and grow a crop, the Kingdom of God will function for anyone who knows how to use the laws of the Kingdom. You are a member of God's household and a citizen of His great Kingdom and have access to all that He has.

So let me tell you why so many of God's people are failing in life. They do not know how the Kingdom of God operates, and they do not know how to hear the Holy Spirit.

Dan's success was not something Dan thought up. It was a unique Holy Spirit strategy that was discerned because Dan took steps to apply Kingdom law, and he and his wife were listening for the Holy Spirit to speak and to help them with a plan.

THE HOLY SPIRIT HAS THE PLAN!

—Your Financial Revolution: The Power of Strategy

Week 25: Ask God for the Plan

Prayer Focus

Ask God to show you what you have in your possession for Him to work with. Thank Him for new direction, new ideas, and new concepts by revelation.

Think on It

→ Have you ever been incorrectly disillusioned with God or wrongly blamed Him for your troubles?

→ Do you believe that God's promises are for your life as much as they're for everyone else?

→ Do you believe you can hear the Holy Spirit?

Pursue Change

Jesus taught us how to release the Kingdom into the earth realm, and we learn the same from Dan's story in the excerpt.

This week, take a look at what you have in your possession. What do you have in your life that you can give God to work with? Jesus multiplied bread into bread and fish into fish. What do you need multiplied in your life? Find some of it.

Remember that money can be named. You don't sow money to believe for paper. Money represents your life and can be named to be the thing you need multiplied.

Next, make sure you're in faith, then confess over what you have, and release it in faith.

Expect the plan from God. The Holy Spirit will give you new direction, new ideas, and new concepts by revelation. Carry a notepad and a pen. Write everything down.

Then, when God gives you the plan, MOVE!

Notes

Week 26

Don't Hand Over the Keys

I will give you the keys of the kingdom of heaven; whatever you bind on earth will be bound in heaven, and whatever you loose on earth will be loosed in heaven.
—Matthew 16:19

"Every single day, we have two choices: We can simply react to everything happening around us, or we can take action and create the lives we want to live."

—*Shark Proof*

After decades of marriage, raising a family, ministry, and business, I've learned a POWERFUL lesson...

How to be HAPPY.

You're probably thinking, *That's crazy, Drenda! Everyone knows how to be happy!*

Sure, I knew how to be happy when I got my way and life was going right... but what about when everything was going terribly WRONG?

What about when sharks (people with wrong motives) were attacking me left and right? Or when I was living in an old farmhouse that had plants growing through the windows, I was digging through couch cushions to find enough money to get the kids McDonald's, and I found out bees had set up their home in the bedroom my sons shared?

Making the choice to rejoice and walking in freedom wasn't so easy on those days.

I remember going through the drive-through with my children one day, and I was stressed, tired, and worried about different circumstances with sharks in Gary's and my lives. If you've ever gone through the drive-through with five little ones in your vehicle, you know the ordering process can be frustrating. I tried my best to order as each child loudly chimed in, in unison, with their order.

Week 26: Don't Hand Over the Keys

The McDonald's worker handed me our food, and I pulled away. The smell of french fries filled the car, and my worries started to fade as I grew more excited to eat. I drove down the road and pulled over where we could enjoy our meal in the car.

I handed each child a meal, but as I went to pull mine out, my hand reached the bottom of the bag.

They forgot my food!

Now I was stressed, tired, and HANGRY. Yes, that is a real emotion! I raised the cup of Sprite in my hand in a burst of anger; and as if on cue, the lid on the paper cup popped open, sending a small tidal wave of Sprite all over the car. My kids watched in silent awe, and I heard my oldest daughter, Amy, start to cry.

I looked up at the Sprite-stained roof of our van with the soundtrack of my daughter softly crying in the back seat. I had totally blown it.

We all have bad days, but you don't have to let your circumstances keep you from walking in the freedom you have in Christ. I learned how to make the choice to rejoice the hard way, but you don't have to!

> *"Be selective with your battles. Sometimes peace is better than being right."*
>
> —Anonymous

I realized that I needed to change my mindset. It was time to shut down the pity party for one. I put up a sign in our bathroom that said, "Make the choice to rejoice." Every time I started to feel bad for myself, I went into the bathroom and read that sign.

Then I looked at myself in the mirror and gave myself a little pep talk. *"Drenda, this isn't your forever... You're going to bigger and better places! You can do it! You were made for this!"*

I regained my joy and took back my day!

The powerful lesson I learned was that my happiness was MY CHOICE. I could CHOOSE to have a good day—to be unaffected by screaming toddlers, a difficult person at work, or something somebody said that was intended to wound me.

It was an incredible discovery: I was the master of my emotions.

Nobody can steal your joy unless YOU give them permission.

Every single day, we have two choices: We can simply react to everything happening around us, or we can take action and create the lives we want to live. If we put our happiness in other people's hands, we're going to be disappointed. Not only that, but we'll be on an emotional roller coaster.

Week 26: Don't Hand Over the Keys

Don't give someone else the keys to your happiness!

It's incredibly freeing when we take back the responsibility for how we feel. When we react to others' actions, it sets us up to be the victim. When we maintain the fact that we own our emotions, we free ourselves to be victorious in all circumstances!

Just like Matthew 16:19 says, the keys are in your hands. What are you going to do with them?

—Shark Proof

Prayer Focus

Thank God that He has given you the keys to the Kingdom and the power to bind and loose here on Earth. Ask Him to help you always remember that no one and no thing can steal your joy unless you let them/it.

Think on It

→ Do you know how to be happy?

→ Are you more likely to be unhappy when you're stressed, tired, or hungry?

→ When was the last time you had a pity party? Why?

Pursue Change

This is the week to start taking responsibility for how you feel. You, and only you, own your emotions. You are the master of your own happiness. Don't allow yourself to have any more pity parties or to react to everything happening around you. Instead, take action and create the life you want to live.

Notes

Week 27
Use Your Authority

This is the confidence we have in approaching God: that if we ask anything according to his will, he hears us. And if we know that he hears us—whatever we ask—we know that we have what we asked of him.

—1 John 5:14-15

"What are you saying? With every word (you speak), you are setting in motion spiritual law!"

—*Your Financial Revolution: The Power of Provision*

Believing in your heart or having faith is not the end of the equation. As we have already seen, when you believe what heaven says, you are justified. It is now legal for heaven to flow into the earth realm, but nothing happens until you release that authority into the earth realm. You are seated with Christ in heavenly places on the right hand of the Father. Your words are the words of a king, and heaven cannot be released here until you speak! This can be a declaration or an agreement spoken in prayer, but you hold the keys of the Kingdom. God cannot do it without you!

It is not just a matter of knowing how to go through the action of praying that makes things happen; it is knowing to give a directive when you do so. Remember, if you do not loose heaven here in the earth, it will not be done. So it is imperative that we understand how to loose heaven's will into our lives and our world.

One of the best examples of giving a directive is taught in the Lord's Prayer. There are some major keys here in the Lord's Prayer you need to be aware of. First, the text says that God already knows what you need, so stop the begging. Begging is not faith, and it shows ignorance relative to how the Kingdom works and your rights as a citizen of the Kingdom. Giving a directive in prayer is really making a requisition. A requisition is a very detailed list of what you need. It is not asking for those items; it is laying claim to those items.

Week 27: Use Your Authority

> *And when you pray, do not keep on babbling like pagans, for they think they will be heard because of their many words. Do not be like them, for your Father knows what you need before you ask him. This, then, is how you should pray: "Our Father in heaven, hallowed be your name, your kingdom come, your will be done, on earth as it is in heaven. Give us today our daily bread."*
>
> —Matthew 6:7-11

Jesus starts off with, "*Our Father in heaven, hallowed [greatly revered and honored] be your name [reflecting on His dominion and authority].*" Jesus is setting the legal posture of prayer in this first sentence.

Next, the Lord's Prayer says, "*Your kingdom come, your will be done.*"

This phrase is putting a demand on the court to rule according to the law of the Kingdom. You are about to make a request or bring an issue to the court, and you are asking the Judge to enforce what His will (the law) says in regard to this case. Next it says, "*On earth as it is in heaven.*" Again, you are stating that you want this ruling in heaven to be enforced on Earth as it is in heaven. Now, all of this was to establish and posture you and the court. Nothing has been asked or presented yet. But next comes the petition.

"*Give us today our daily bread.*" This statement really does not have much to do with bread unless that is exactly what you need. Instead, it is telling you to insert what it is you need. Remember, this whole conversation began where Jesus was instructing His disciples how to pray to get their needs met. This is where you make your petition, but as I said, a better word to be used here is requisition.

Of course, both will work, and petition is what Philippians 4 says. But the point I want to get across is a petition is a detailed request. The point to remember is detailed. You are giving a directive in prayer; it has to be detailed and exact. Philippians 4:6-7 tell us the same thing.

> *Do not be anxious about anything, but in every situation, by prayer and petition, with thanksgiving, present your requests to God. And the peace of God, which transcends all understanding, will guard your hearts and your minds in Christ Jesus.*

Notice that prayers and petitions are different. Our prayers carry our petitions, but prayers are the vehicles that take them to our Father. Again, a petition is very detailed and precise. But most Christians would say something like this, "Oh, whatever God wants to bring me is fine. He knows best." Wrong, Wrong, Wrong!

God has given YOU the keys of the Kingdom!

—*Your Financial Revolution: The Power of Provision*

Week 27: Use Your Authority

Prayer Focus

Thank God that He gave us the perfect model for prayer. Pray the Lord's Prayer from Matthew 6.

Think on It

→ Do you approach God with confidence, believing that He hears you? Why or why not?

→ Do you have a tendency to beg God?

→ Do you make detailed and precise requests of God? Why or why not?

Pursue Change

Prayer is more than speaking; it's also *listening*.

This week, pray the Lord's Prayer over your life, and then get quiet and listen for what God has to say. You may find that being still and listening are weaknesses in your prayer life that need work.

Notes

Notes

Week 28

Renew Your Mind

Consequently, faith comes from hearing the message, and the message is heard through the word about Christ.

—Romans 10:17

"You have to get a fresh vision for life. You have to renew your mind morning, day, and night. Take what was pain, what was trauma, what was discouragement, and renew the picture to match God's promises."

—*Better Than You Think*

When obsessive thoughts come up, you have to replace them with Scripture. When negative thinking comes against you, you have to replace those negative thoughts with positive ones. When problems come, remember the promise.

The culture can medicate you outwardly with antidepressants, but you need the emotional healing that only comes from God. The world isn't equipped to reach you in the places you need reached. The only things the world can do are numb and harden emotions with alcohol, medications, pleasure, and sin. Counseling may give you the ability to cope with things in the soul realm (mind, will, and emotions), but ultimately, your true freedom comes from your time in His presence with His Word and prayer.

> *The Lord is close to the brokenhearted and saves those who are crushed in spirit.*
> —Psalm 34:18

People have said to us, "Oh, you and Gary have the Midas touch. Anything you touch just prospers and is blessed." Trust me, it did not use to be that way!

Gary and I spent nine years living hand-to-mouth, paycheck-to-paycheck. We not only owed thousands to the bank and maxed out our credit there, but we also owed thousands to our relatives.

Week 28: Renew Your Mind

When we were going through tough times, I put Scriptures everywhere: the bathroom, our bedroom, and the kitchen. Why did I do that? I had to remember that I wasn't staying in the wilderness forever. We were going through a hard time, but we were going through—we were not staying there.

I was headed to somewhere else, somewhere better. God had a promise for my family and for me. He was taking me somewhere. I was not always going to live in that captivity. I was set free in my spirit, and the Word of God was working on my mind. I was learning how to access the Kingdom inside of me by renewing my mind.

Put Scriptures wherever you tend to go when you're in that foggy state of mind. I used to run to the bathroom when I felt depressed or when I was throwing a pity party. It was my one quiet place, so I put Scriptures there.

Renew your mind by:
    1. Hearing the Word of God
    2. Reading the Word of God
    3. Speaking the Word of God

Listen to the Word of God. Put on our *Better Than You Think* Scripture CD, and intentionally meditate on those truths while you are going throughout your day. Read your Bible out loud so you are speaking and hearing the Word of God. Replace your negative thinking with thoughts of the hope and future God has for you!

Changing the picture

It starts with the Word of God. Reading the Word of God without grabbing hold of it isn't enough. Your spirit and your mind have to come into agreement with the Word. They have to come together in agreement, and then come out of your mouth. Out of the abundance of the heart, the mouth speaks it (Luke 6:45). That's how you receive the promises of God! That's how you find a new vision for your life!

Quit rehearsing the past. You can't live thinking about what you did yesterday. You have to forgive whomever, whatever, and get a new vision from God that will paint a new picture of hope for your life. You have to believe that God's Word is bigger than your thoughts, your experiences, or what you've been through. God's love has more healing ability than anything that has happened to you!

Put your focus on what is right. I have to say this, and it may sound harsh, but depression results from a focus on self. It is focused on what happened to self. It is focused on protecting oneself. A depressed person isn't thinking about what God says or thinks about the issue but, rather, is thinking about how they feel about the problem. These thoughts become the constant focus until the person shuts themselves off from life and others. They are problem focused, not promise focused.

Week 28: Renew Your Mind

Stay accountable. You need somebody to hold you accountable not to speak negative words over your life. When someone is depressed, they think depressive thoughts, they rehearse depressing things, and then they speak negative things over their life. Those negative thoughts become negative words.

Take captive every thought and stronghold and subject them to the Word of God.

—*Better Than You Think*

Prayer Focus

Thank God for giving you a clear path to build faith—hearing the Word of God. Ask Him to help you be consistently passionate about hearing, reading, and speaking His Word.

Think on It

→ Do you replace negative thoughts with positive ones?

→ Do you regularly renew your mind by hearing, reading, and speaking the Word of God, or do you fail to do one or more of these three things regularly?

→ Where has your focus been in the last 30 days? Does it need to change?

Pursue Change

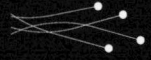

This week, access the Kingdom inside of you by renewing your mind as shared in this week's book excerpt:

> Listen to the Word of God. Intentionally meditate on those truths while you are going throughout your day. Read your Bible out loud so you are speaking and hearing the Word of God. Replace your negative thinking with thoughts of the hope and future God has for you.

Follow the steps listed in this week's book excerpt to change your picture and take every thought captive.

Notes

Week 29

Partner with God

Week 29: Partner with God

I thank my God every time I remember you. In all my prayers for all of you, I always pray with joy because of your partnership in the gospel from the first day until now, being confident of this, that he who began a good work in you will carry it on to completion until the day of Christ Jesus. It is right for me to feel this way about all of you, since I have you in my heart and, whether I am in chains or defending and confirming the gospel, all of you share in God's grace with me.

—Philippians 1:3-7

"Partnership is a powerful spiritual principle you will want to be aware of and take advantage of."
—*Your Financial Revolution: The Power of Generosity*

I have been in the financial business for almost 40 years now. Through the years, I have had many people ask me how to start businesses and what makes a business grow.

Of course, there are many things people need to know, but the most important thing I could tell them is that they need a partner.

Now, as a pastor for many years, I have seen more than my share of people who thought it would be great to go into business with their church buddy, and then the whole thing imploded. Friends get offended by each other, and many times even stop talking, and the relationship is ruined. Because I have seen this so many times, I rarely suggest that you go into business with your friend unless you have the boundaries clearly laid out and written out.

However, there is a partner that I always insist you take on, and that is God.

We talked (before) about the woman who received the prophet Elijah and gave him her last meal. We saw how that act of faith produced food every day for the prophet, God's assignment, and the woman's family. She partnered with him in his assignment, and in so doing, the anointing and provision that were on his assignment became hers. They were partners.

The definition of partner is: A person who shares or is

Week 29: Partner with God

associated with another in some action or endeavor; usually sharing its risks and profits. A partnership is a legal entity and shares in the risks, costs, and profit of the business.[4]

So, when Peter gave Jesus the boat to use (in Luke 5), he was really loaning Jesus the business in a legal sense, not just the boat. Technically, James and John also owned a part of the boat that Peter let Jesus use, and because of their partnership, both boats filled equally.

James and John reaped exactly the same harvest as Peter did even though they did not exercise faith in that situation at all. I bet they were glad that Peter was their partner that day.

In Philippians 1:3-7, Paul says he remembers the church at Philippi with joy because of their continuing partnership with his ministry. He goes on to state that, because of their partnership, they now shared in God's grace that was on his ministry.

Grace is God's empowerment or God's ability that was on Paul to accomplish his assignment. The church at Philippi was sharing the expense of the assignment, and, like James and John, they also shared in the anointing and grace that was on that assignment.

Now let's go over to chapter four, and you will see the

---

[4] https://www.collinsdictionary.com/us/dictionary/english.

amazing result that partnership produces.

> *Yet it was good of you to share in my troubles. Moreover, as you Philippians know, in the early days of your acquaintance with the gospel, when I set out from Macedonia, not one church shared with me in the matter of giving and receiving, except you only; for even when I was in Thessalonica, you sent me aid more than once when I was in need. Not that I desire your gifts; what I desire is that more be credited to your account. I have received full payment and have more than enough. I am amply supplied, now that I have received from Epaphroditus the gifts you sent. They are a fragrant offering, an acceptable sacrifice, pleasing to God. And my God will meet all your needs according to the riches of his glory in Christ Jesus.*
> —Philippians 4:14-19

Paul had just received another contribution from the Philippian church. Listen to what he says back to them. "*My God will meet all your needs.*"

Notice that Paul did not say, "Your God will meet your needs because you have been generous to me." NO! He said, "Now, MY God will meet your needs!"

You see, the Philippians were partners with Paul, and as partners, they shared in that grace that was on Paul's assignment. Now, like James and John catching all those

Week 29: Partner with God

fish because of Peter's faith, Paul is declaring that their needs will be met because of his faith!

I hope you can see the advantage of this principle.

—*Your Financial Revolution: The Power of Generosity*

Prayer Focus

Thank God for giving you mentors, leaders, and partners who share with you what they've learned about the Kingdom of God and His promises and provide ideas, support, experience, and wisdom to help you capture the opportunities God has for you.

Think on It

→ Are you in partnership with anyone?

→ Is anything preventing you from taking advantage of the Kingdom principle of partnership?

→ How can you partner with God?

Pursue Change

This week, evaluate your "partnerships." Ask God if anything should change.

God gave us Paul as a very clear example of the importance of partnership in the Bible. He gave Paul the directive to travel and preach the Gospel, but Paul's God-given assignment was too big for him to do on his own. He needed prayers and financial support. He needed *partners*.

Paul was overjoyed that the church at Philippi partnered with him. As his partners, they shared in the responsibility of helping him accomplish God's assignment. Paul tells them in Philippians 1:5-7 that the same grace that God gave *him* was shared with *them* because of their partnership. That's incredibly powerful.

Matthew 10:40-42 also tell us that, because of their partnership, they would share in the same reward that Paul would receive for being faithful to his assignment.

Notes

Week 30

Don't Be Ruled by Feelings

I can do all this through him who gives me strength.

—Philippians 4:13

"Whether we realize it or not, almost every decision we make is weighed against our vision."

—*Better Than You Feel*

"I don't feel like working today."

"I don't feel like I love my spouse anymore."

"I don't want to be their friend!"

Feelings that rule our lives will also rule our success. We better make sure they are not only based in truth but also that if we succumb to the feelings we are experiencing, they are going to cause us to end up where we want to go! I have seen people give in to the feeling that they didn't want to work, resulting in their family becoming destitute financially.

There is a powerful connection between vision, desire, and feelings. What would it be like to feel inspired to work and to accomplish a triumphant feat that you were proud of? Let yourself imagine or dream a big dream. Vision paints a picture of a desired end. We are admonished to write the vision and make it plain in Habakkuk 2:2. And at the same time, people perish or quit if there is no vision.

Temptations and distractions present themselves constantly and challenge our resolve and goals. It's easy to take the path of instant gratification, but if my vision speaks of something greater, a burning desire will fuel my emotions, and the self-control from God's Spirit will enable me to do all things through Christ.

Health and weight loss are great examples. If I picture the

Week 30: Don't Be Ruled by Feelings

short term, I may choose to eat the chocolate cake because I see it, and then I get a burning desire to eat it. But if I see a bigger vision and think about vacation, swimsuit, and healthy lifestyle, my burning desire is now for something beyond the moment. I say, "No cake for me today!" or "Only one bite!" I feel motivated to stay focused on my goal. Whether we realize it or not, almost every decision we make is weighed against our vision.

If we don't feel like working, we probably have lost vision (or perhaps never had one) that the reward is greater than the immediate lure of the alternative—sleep, watching television, gaming, or eating. "A little sleep, a little slumber, a little folding of the hands to rest—and poverty will come on you like a thief" (Proverbs 24:33-34a). Thieves steal and take something unlawfully. How is lack of vision and a burning desire stealing the future from a generation of sleepers?

In the area of relationships, I have seen people pull away from church or friendships because they feel hurt or offended by something that happened. Many years of valuable investment and rewards of enjoyable exchanges can be lost because of feelings of offense. Inevitably, if you confront the silence or impenetrable walls and ask if something is wrong or if they are offended, they almost always say, "No," but their actions indicate otherwise.

The vision to continue in a relationship must dictate our actions rather than a momentary problem. It's pretty shortsighted and emotionally immature to think that we can have a relationship where there is not an occasional offense or misunderstanding. If we have false expectations of relationships, we will be disappointed. Our actions can sabotage what could be a meaningful and deeper friendship if we don't have the emotional security and foresight to stay with the big picture instead of the momentary challenge.

What does our will have to do with living lives of peace, joy, and prosperous relationships and finances? Everything!

Who's in control of our lives? And how powerful is our will to get something accomplished? I grew up with the phrase, "Where there's a will, there's a way." And although it's true, we can pursue our own will to our own harm! After I committed my life to God, I made the decision I would live by the reformed statement, "Where there's God's will, there's a way."

Anchor your choices to truth based on God's Word, or emotions will rule your life.

When you and I are pressed mentally and emotionally but decide to forfeit our will for the Father's, we take on His will, and we, therefore, take on His grace! God gives us the power, or anointing, to do the thing we could not do ourselves.

—*Better Than You Feel*

Week 30: Don't Be Ruled by Feelings

Prayer Focus

Ask God to help you always keep a vision of your greater future in front of you so you don't get sidetracked by feelings, temptations, or distractions.

Think on It

→ Is there any area of your life that you realize you've allowed to be ruled by your feelings?

→ When you make decisions, do you weigh them against where you want to be in the future?

→ What do you need to do this week that you've been putting off because you haven't "felt" like doing it?

Pursue Change

This week, reread the book excerpt every day and ask God to show you any areas of your life where you have allowed feelings, temptations, distractions, or your own will to keep you from moving forward into the future He has for you.

Do you need to change your schedule; cut out a certain food or drink; start exercising; stop watching a certain show; or have a conversation with someone you may have offended, or someone who offended you? Listen for the Holy Spirit's direction and take action.

Notes

Notes

Week 31

Live at Rest

There remains, then, a Sabbath-rest for the people of God; for anyone who enters God's rest also rests from their works, just as God did from his. Let us, therefore, make every effort to enter that rest, so that no one will fall by following their example of disobedience.

—Hebrews 4:9-11

"Drenda and I lived a life of torment, fear, sickness, and insecurity for nine long years until we found that the Sabbath rest was in fact an option for our lives. I am serious!"

—*Your Financial Revolution: The Power of Rest*

What if there really was a way to live life in perpetual Sabbath? How awesome it would be if there really was a way to live life free from fear, full of provision, full of purpose, and living in a place of rest!

There is a Sabbath rest available for the people of God today. Hebrews 4:9-11 imply that we can enter into God's rest and rest from our work. Remember what we just studied: God's rest says everything is whole, complete, and provision is readily available. There is freedom from the survival mentality, freedom from being imprisoned by poverty, and freedom from sickness and disease. There are new options! The Sabbath was not just Old Testament information; it is for us today as well. But before you think I am talking about living under all the Old Testament legalism and rituals again, I am not. Instead, I want to examine this Sabbath rest that Hebrews talks about. Because as Drenda and I have found out, herein lies a very important key to the Kingdom of God functioning and providing in our lives as God intended.

SHOCKER: THE SABBATH IS NOT A DAY ANY LONGER!

I hope that statement got your attention. There has been great discussion in the body of Christ as to how the Sabbath should be celebrated: Saturday, Sunday, or beginning at sundown on Friday night until sundown on Saturday evening. Whole denominations have been built around their interpretation of the Sabbath. Before you throw this

Week 31: Live at Rest

book across the room in disgust thinking I am a heretic, please bear with me for just a moment, and let's take a look at Colossians 2:16-17:

> *Therefore do not let anyone judge you by what you eat or drink, or with regard to a religious festival, a New Moon celebration or a Sabbath day. These are a shadow of the things that were to come; the reality, however, is found in Christ.*

Pay close attention to what Paul says. The Sabbath day was a shadow of the things that were to come; the reality, however, is found in Christ. The Sabbath day was a shadow; it was not the real thing. If Christ is the real thing, then the Sabbath day was a shadow of who He is and what He did. Let me say it this way: There is no power in the Sabbath day to take away or change the earth curse system of painful toil and sweat that Adam brought into the earth realm. If you religiously honor it, by itself and of itself, it has no power to set you free. But it is a shadow, a picture, of what you will find in Christ.

Its shadow said to not work, no painful toil and sweat. It was only a shadow, however, not the real thing. But it was pointing to Jesus Christ, who has, in fact, set us free from the curse of the law and the earth curse system and reestablished us as sons and daughters of God and citizens of God's great Kingdom! Again, it was a picture of what Jesus would bring back to us someday. It is a finished work where everything we need for life has been restored back to us. However, as Hebrews says, we enter into this rest through faith. Remember, faith is required to make it legal for heaven to have jurisdiction here in the earth realm. On the cross Jesus cried out, "It is finished!" just as God said it was finished at the end of the sixth day.

The Sabbath for most people today is a religious day. People look upon the Sabbath as God's day, a day where we owe it to God to go to church, do stuff for God, and do other religious things. Jesus had to correct His disciples, who had the same mindset.

> *The Sabbath was made for man, not man for the Sabbath.*
> —Mark 2:27b

The shadow of the Sabbath day says it is forbidden for you to toil and sweat for what you need on the Sabbath day, but it was only giving us a glimpse of what Jesus did, which was free us from the earth curse system of having to toil and sweat to survive. In other words, what it pictured became the reality in Christ.

—*Your Financial Revolution: The Power of Rest*

Week 31: Live at Rest

Prayer Focus

Thank God for sending Jesus, the true Sabbath, and that in Him we find access to the Kingdom of God and all that it has. Thus, we can rest!

Think on It

→ Do you believe it's truly possible to live life free from fear, full of provision, full of purpose, and living in a place of rest? Why or why not?

→ How have your beliefs about the Sabbath changed?

→ What would an ideal Sabbath Day or Sabbath Life look like for you?

Pursue Change

This week, pray and ask God to give you a clearer understanding than ever before of what the Sabbath rest truly is and how you can live in it. Thank Him that He has already given you everything you need to live in the Sabbath rest. Ask Him to open your eyes and reveal to you exactly where you need to gather the fragments you've been missing, and to help you to never miss an idea, a divine appointment, or a single direction the Holy Spirit is giving you so you can fully capture your double portion.

Consider rereading *Your Financial Revolution: The Power of Rest*, or reading it if you haven't already.

Notes

Notes

Week 32
Communicate Successfully

"If our preconceived idea is that something is true, we will keep looking for the evidence that we're right."

—*Nasty Gets Us Nowhere*

Each person brings different abilities into the marriage and working relationship. Communication is key to vision casting, setting goals, and strategizing how to reach them by determining who will do what when. Honestly, when Gary and I started in business 38 years ago, we couldn't see all that we see today, but we saw pieces of it. And we didn't have a plan all written out for how or who. We both studied the business, attended meetings together, and started to jump into doing whatever was necessary to win.

Vision is exciting, and moving closer toward our dreams inspired us to deal with whatever personal struggles we had to tackle to make it. Dreams fuel your life, and faith fuels your dreams. Our faith in God's Word and in each other made all the financial struggle surmountable. We were just one day closer to our common goals. I discovered my passions and gifts in serving our vision. We both became better because of the value we learned to place on each other.

Saying "I do" is not a guarantee there won't be conflict. You can expect there will be! That's just common sense. Magical pixie dust doesn't fall out of the sky to ensure you're never going to disagree, argue, or battle occasionally. Just don't let it become a war. War presumes the other person's motives and character are villainous and that they are about to strike. You live in a defensive posture if you believe this, waiting for the attack. No relationship, let alone a marriage, can survive in a war zone like this. You can live in pressure

Week 32: Communicate Successfully

and battle outside in a war zone, but you can't believe that the person you live with is the enemy!

People who have lived through real wars have managed to keep their marriages intact. They did so by pulling together and recognizing that the real enemy was not their spouse but was a much greater, more sinister force from outside. That's the protective shield we must fight with if we are to succeed. We must keep the darkness out and reject anything that tries to come against our love for our marriage partner.

Did Gary and I ever have conflict? Of course! And occasionally, we still do. But it's met with much more maturity and understanding today.

I would say the beginning of a vision and its fruition are the best parts of the journey. There are some sticky situations in the middle that can be the hardest, because you are working but aren't seeing the outcome you'd like. That's the pressure point when it's tempting to argue or blame the other person for the pressure. But we need to decide that we are not going to allow arguments to divide us. We can learn to disagree without demands or division.

What words are we speaking, and what dreams are created or destroyed by the power of our words? Words come from the heart, and the heart gets pictures from what we meditate on. The messages we hear and pictures we see form our thoughts. Are we listening to the popular fads or timeless truths? Think and speak God's thoughts and promises to begin to change your communication.

Every couple has a mission. They just haven't always taken the time to get in touch with each other to discover it. What did you dream of doing? What has taken the place of your dream? How can you find it again? So often, conflict occurs because we lose sight of our dreams together. It's amazing how fast we can throw aside our differences when the vision speaks louder. Too many couples are bored with life and become bored with each other because they're not out saving the day together.

There are some keys that will help you communicate successfully. Recognize that if you jump to conclusions quickly, they most always will be flawed, or your response will be way off even if your conclusion is accurate. Slow down and hear the facts or feelings of the other person before you decide. Each sex and individual person has filters they hear through and ways they communicate.

Developing communication that is consistent and inviting stops misunderstandings and helps you both realize your passion and satisfaction. We are really managing personalities and differences for success. The effort is worth the reward.

—Nasty Gets Us Nowhere

Week 32: Communicate Successfully

Prayer Focus

Ask God for His help in developing communication that is consistent and inviting and stops misunderstandings. Thank Him for giving you grace in your conversations and for helping you handle disagreements before they become arguments.

Think on It

→ Would you say you're a good communicator? Why or why not?

→ Do other people in your life think you're a good communicator? Why or why not?

→ Do you believe you can truly agree to disagree with a person and maintain a relationship? Why or why not?

Pursue Change

This week, bite your tongue and don't speak phrases like, "You always..." or "You never...," which immediately put the other person on the defensive. Make every effort to listen more, talk less, and not jump to conclusions or assume that you know what other people are thinking.

If your communication with someone starts to get frustrating, step away for a minute, take a time-out, pray, and then make an effort to discuss your differences of opinion.

Remember, good communication requires time, effort, understanding, and avoiding attitudes or phrases that create conflict or cause the other person to clam up and go silent. The goal is to create unity and, ultimately, good relationships and decision-making, not winning the conversation. Nothing positive comes from threats, control, belittling, or trying to put the other person in their place.

Notes

Week 33
Stop Begging God

You made them a little lower than the angels; you crowned them with glory and honor and put everything under their feet.

In putting everything under them, God left nothing that is not subject to them.
— Hebrews 2:7-8a

"Heaven has no jurisdiction here in the earth realm unless it is through a man or woman who looses it here. That is why Jesus is saying here that if a man or a woman will release heaven's authority here, heaven will back it up. If we don't, heaven can't."
—*Your Financial Revolution: The Power of Allegiance*

Unfortunately, many church people do not know how to tap into the Kingdom of God and receive their answers either. A story in Matthew (17:14-20) illustrates how many think.

In this story, we see a man who is desperate; his son is being tormented by evil spirits, almost to the point of death. Hearing of Jesus's ministry and that Jesus had the power to cast out demons, he made plans to take his son to Jesus so that He could heal him. However, when he got there, he found out that Jesus was not there but had taken three of His disciples up on the mountain to pray. The other disciples who were there said it was no problem; they had been casting out demons ever since Jesus gave them the authority to do so, in His name, and could take care of the man's son. But as they prayed for this young man, the demon did not leave. Although they tried, the demon would not leave. The father was upset, and the crowd that followed Jesus was confused.

But just at that moment, Jesus and the three disciples come down from the mountain and arrive on the scene. Jesus, seeing the commotion, asks what is going on. The father of the son explains how he had brought the boy to the disciples, but they could not cast the demon out. The father then does what will ring true for many, if not most, people facing a crisis whenever there seems to be no answer. He cries out to Jesus for mercy. Although begging for mercy sounds like a good thing to do when you are desperate, it was not this

Week 33: Stop Begging God

man's answer, and it is not yours either. The father, wanting to evoke Jesus's compassion for his situation, then goes on to tell Jesus how the demon has been tormenting his son, throwing him in the fire, and trying to kill him.

Jesus stops the man. He does not need to hear more of the torment the man's son has been enduring. In frustration Jesus cries out, "Oh perverse and unbelieving generation, how long must I put up with you? Bring the boy to me." In His one sentence, Jesus completely explains why the demon did not come out.

But before we dig into the implications of what Jesus said, we need to reaffirm the foundation we rest on, which is that God does not and cannot lie. What He says is true. With that settled, we can assess the situation with this statement, "Demons are SUPPOSED to come out!" If they don't, then there is something wrong, and it is not on God's end but ours. Remember this: The problem with receiving from God is always on our end. Jesus clearly tells us the reason the demon did not leave—perverse thinking and unbelief.

The father was obviously desperate for his son. When nothing seemed to happen when the disciples prayed for him, there was only one thing left to do, and that was to beg for mercy. The phrase "begging for mercy" implies that someone has the power or authority to help but has chosen not to do so.

Quite frankly, this is how most people pray. Knowing that God has the power to help but uncertain of His response, they beg for mercy. So with long prayers and many words, they lay out the details of their pain and circumstances. "Father, you know I need that money by Friday. Please, God, help me." Or "God, please, if you heal my child, I will serve you all the days of my life. Please, God."

I am not making light of the situations that people face, but please make note of how quickly Jesus brought the power of God to bear in that situation and freed the boy. This is God's heart, His desire. There is no shortage of compassion, power, or authority. That was not the problem in the story either. Jesus laid out the problem as perverse thinking and unbelief. In other words, wrong thinking and their lack of faith hindered the Kingdom's jurisdiction in this case.

—Your Financial Revolution: The Power of Allegiance

Week 33: Stop Begging God

Prayer Focus

Thank God for His heart and desire to bring His power into every situation and see people FREE. Ask Him to correct any wrong thinking or lack of faith you have that is hindering His power from working in your life.

Think on It

→ What have you previously thought about this story from Matthew 17?

→ Do you use your God-given authority in situations in your life? If so, how? If not, why?

→ Do you have a hard time believing that everything in the Bible is still for today? Why or why not?

Pursue Change

You have authority in the Kingdom. You have position, being seated with Christ in heavenly realms (Ephesians 2:6). And, you know what? If you're seated with Christ, that makes you a *king* in the earth realm. And kings *rule*!

Kings *decree*, or *speak*, to get things done.

This week, start acting like the king (or queen) God has made you in the earth realm. RULE over Satan! Set the captives free and declare the good news of His Kingdom to everyone!

Notes

_____

_____

_____

_____

_____

_____

Notes

Week 34

Ask Yourself These Questions

that battle within you? You desire but do not have, so you kill. You covet but you cannot get what you want, so you quarrel and fight. You do not have because you do not ask God. When you ask, you do not receive, because you ask with wrong motives, that you may spend what you get on your pleasures.

—James 4:1-3

"Lasting change and freedom only come from the power of God working in us when we invite Jesus to be Lord of our lives."

—*Shark Proof*

No one can steal our peace or joy from us unless we allow it. We are responsible for our lives, our decisions, and our choices. I had to analyze why I was always trying to "fix" things to my own harm. When you step into enabling or taking false responsibility, eventually, you break down emotionally and physically. These are questions I had to ask myself, and I encourage you to do the same.

- Who is responsible for the issue? (responsibility)

- Who ultimately has the authority to solve the problem? (authority)

- How am I hindering their change? (accountability)

- What is my motive for helping? (motive)

When I asked myself these questions, I realized much of my life had been spent taking false responsibility for solving problems that I did not have the God-given authority to fix. Was I doing this because I wanted to be loved, admired, or appreciated? Was I getting my identity from performing or from the Lord Jesus Christ? How many times had this controlled my life, my joy, my peace? All of the times I had cried myself to sleep because someone I had helped had stuck a dagger in my back were due to a lack of understanding of where my responsibility started and stopped. I recognized that love deficits in my own heart had caused me to perform for love instead of just obeying God.

Week 34: Ask Yourself These Questions

How many times had I neglected my responsibility to God, myself, or my family while trying to be superwoman to others? How many times had I gotten in the way of someone making real change happen in their lives because I thought that "good Christians" who were successful were obligated to fix everyone's problems? How many times had I caused people I loved to not reap the consequences of a life-changing lesson because I played their savior instead of letting Jesus assume that role in their lives? Ouch!

Sometimes my motives were right, but my choice was wrong. And sometimes my motives were wrong—to get something someone couldn't give me, self-worth. God has healed many wounds in my heart and restored places that were devastated by goats, wolves… and sharks! I have had to learn that I must be at the command of the Lord, not the dictates of people, pressures, or my own issues. If you are giving to a shark, look out! You are casting your pearls… to be trampled and eaten.

So often in life, the bites we receive are from someone who has been bitten. We have all bitten others ourselves! I think of the lyrics by Art Garfunkel: "I bruise you. You bruise me. We all bruise so easily." Misunderstandings and the lack of empathy for what another person is dealing with may be the biggest contributors to relationship rifts and difficult situations.

I constantly hear from disillusioned leaders and heartbroken pastors who are ready to quit because someone they have loved or invested in has wounded or left them. I encourage them not to abort the mission because of a lost friend or team member. Although some relationships will not be repaired, there are encouraging stories of restoration when we choose to grow and stay the course. Trust can be broken, but it also has the potential to be rebuilt.

When we stop controlling or taking false responsibility for people's decisions, they are free to decide, and the Holy Spirit can work in our hearts to keep priorities straight.

Is everyone who bites a shark? No. They've possibly been bitten by sharks themselves and may mistake you for the predator! There is restoration in Christ, but each person has to want it sincerely enough to be humble before God, seek the truth, and accept personal responsibility. If we can't have empathy for others or communicate honestly, real relationship cannot exist. Before any of us write off others as sharks, let's examine our own hearts and responsibility. God is looking for fruit in our lives and integrity in our hearts. That is always our responsibility.

There is hope and healing in God and His affirming love! We may not forget the pain inflicted by life, by our mistakes, or by a goat or wolf (shark), but we can be resolved of feeling

Week 34: Ask Yourself These Questions

its sting in our lives. Even death itself has been swallowed up by the sacrifice of Jesus!

—Shark Proof

Prayer Focus

Ask God to help you be like Jesus, helping meet people's needs while holding them accountable for their own decisions, not taking false responsibility for people's sins or choices.

Think on It

→ How often do you find yourself enabling someone or taking false responsibility?

→ In what area(s) of your life do you feel pressured to "perform" or do things for others in order to receive approval or love?

→ When was the last time you were a "shark" to someone else? Do you need to go and fix anything?

Pursue Change

In Dr. C. Thomas and Maureen Anderson's book, *Name of the Game of Life*, Maureen Anderson discusses three different roles of dysfunctional patterns originating from parental examples and life experiences. These three roles are the victim, the enabler, and the persecutor. The traits of these roles help us to see how we can assume unhealthy attitudes and fall into the sin of idolatry, greed, or legalism in relationships. These are unhealthy ways in which people relate to and use one another to meet needs that only God can fill.

This week, really pay attention to your behaviors and words. Do you take on one of these three dysfunctional roles? Or are you a helper, like Jesus, who encourages, loves, pleases God, and calls people to maturity?

(See *Shark Proof* for detailed descriptions of the dysfunctional roles as well as the helper role.)

Notes

Week 35
Don't Silence Your Conscience

So, as the Holy Spirit says: "Today, if you hear his voice, do not harden your hearts as you did in the rebellion, during the time of testing in the wilderness."

—Hebrews 3:7-8

"Everyone has a conscience. You may disagree. You may know of people that seem to have no feelings. But I guarantee they did not start out there. If a person continues to resist the voice of their conscience, that voice will get quieter and quieter."

—*Your Financial Revolution: The Power of Strategy*

When I begin to teach on the voice of the Holy Spirit, so many people tell me that they have never heard God's voice. But I always tell them, "Yes, you have!" If you feel the same way, that you have never heard God's voice, then please turn to 1 Kings 19:11-12.

> *The Lord said, "Go out and stand on the mountain in the presence of the Lord, for the Lord is about to pass by."*
>
> *Then a great and powerful wind tore the mountains apart and shattered the rocks before the Lord, but the Lord was not in the wind. After the wind there was an earthquake, but the Lord was not in the earthquake. After the earthquake came a fire, but the Lord was not in the fire. And after the fire came a gentle whisper.*
>
> —1 Kings 19:11-12

The normal voice of the Holy Spirit is this gentle whisper. It is a small, still voice. God's voice sounds like a thought with a different twang to it. Here though, I want to talk to you about the voice of God that no one thinks about—but that all have heard.

Like a candle, its light shines to expose the darkness. It keeps a perfect record of every thought and every deed you have ever committed. Like a witness in the courtroom, it testifies to that which is most hidden. It speaks and reminds

Week 35: Don't Silence Your Conscience

you to do what is right and to avoid what is wrong. The conscience is the inner voice of God within each person. The conscience calls each man or woman to account for their actions. The conscience summons each person, as in a courtroom, to give an account before God. As a witness is called upon to give evidence, so our conscience either speaks on our behalf (defends) or condemns (accuses) us.

The conscience is God's voice in every man and woman, an imprint of the Creator and His requirements to live the lives we were created to live. No one can escape their conscience. I used to be amazed that someone that murdered someone or robbed a bank and got away with it would suddenly just turn themselves in. But now I know there is not a greater torment than a conscience that is condemning the person as guilty! Paul says that the conscience testifies, it speaks.

> *Now this is our boast: Our conscience testifies that we have conducted ourselves in the world, and especially in our relations with you, in the holiness and sincerity that are from God. We have done so, relying not on worldly wisdom but on God's grace.*
> —2 Corinthians 1:12

> *(Indeed, when Gentiles, who do not have the law, do by nature things required by the law, they are a law for themselves, even though they do not have the law. They show that the requirements of the law are written on their hearts, their consciences also bearing*

> *witness, and their thoughts sometimes accusing them and at other times even defending them.)*
> —Romans 2:14-15

The conscience cannot make you do anything—it speaks. You can ignore it or go against it. But Paul warns that if you ignore your conscience, it can cause you great trouble or shipwreck your life.

> *Timothy, my son, I am giving you this command in keeping with the prophecies once made about you, so that by recalling them you may fight the battle well, holding on to faith and a good conscience, which some have rejected and so have suffered shipwreck with regard to the faith.*
> —1 Timothy 1:18-19

Basically, people who harden themselves against the voice of their consciences have lost their ability to steer their lives. Their compasses have been damaged and do not work anymore. They cannot tell which way they are going. Paul says we need to hold on to a good conscience, one that is clean, to make sure we are navigating the correct way. Because we can harden our hearts and damage our ability to feel right and wrong.

If you override your conscience, you will harden your heart, and it will be easier to do it the next time, and the next time, and the next time until you can't hear God at all.

Week 35: Don't Silence Your Conscience

And if we allow our hearts to get hard, we become unusable to God.

—*Your Financial Revolution: The Power of Strategy*

Prayer Focus

Thank God for giving you your conscience—His imprint, His voice—inside of you. Repent for any times you have ignored or overridden your conscience, and ask Him to help you to be obedient every time He speaks, no matter how quietly.

Think on It

→ Have you ever silenced your conscience? What happened?

→ Can you think of a time when you absolutely could not ignore your conscience?

→ In what area(s) of your life do you realize you may have been hardening your heart and preventing yourself from hearing God?

Pursue Change

The dictionary defines sleep as a natural and periodic state of rest during which consciousness of the world is suspended.[5] Spiritual sleep is no different. Our consciousness of God is suspended. We have to recognize it before it's too late.

We're all weak. We've all made mistakes. But you don't have to stay there, or get worse.

This is your week to come clean if you need to. Humble yourself before God. Trust Him. Let the Holy Spirit correct you and deal with you.

---

5 https://www.thefreedictionary.com/sleep.

Notes

Notes

Week 36

Break Up with Fear

There is no fear in love. But perfect love drives out fear, because fear has to do with punishment. The one who fears is not made perfect in love.

—1 John 4:18

"Break up with fear once and for all. And when fear tries to come back, when it tries to talk to you, when it tries to find a place in your life, take authority over it."

— *Better Than You Think*

Do you remember your first encounter with fear, what it felt like, looked like, and acted like?

Fear doesn't feel good. You feel out of sorts and uncomfortable, like somebody is restraining you. You can tell just from that first date that fear is a manipulative control freak. But once you have had that first encounter, there is something that draws you back to fear over and over again.

Fear is a counterfeit of love, so it shouldn't surprise us that our bodies respond to fear a lot like an infatuation. Once we get a little taste, it is harder and harder to pull away. And the more time we spend with fear, the more time it demands. Our minds obsess over it and meditate on it!

When you finished a daunting speech or you tried something outside of your comfort zone—how did you feel? Did you feel free, like a weight was lifted off of you?

Let me make something very clear right off: Any relationship you have with fear is an abusive relationship. In a similar way, you can grow codependent on fear and use it as a coping mechanism for situations. *Tolerating* fear, *coping* with fear, and *reacting* to fear are not freedom.

Fear and love cannot coexist; fear will never look out for your best interest. Fear tries to replace God's love in your life.

Week 36: Break Up with Fear

Fear is a counterfeit of love—when we give it a place in our lives, it sets into motion the opposite fruit that God's perfect and unconditional love does. Any relationship with fear is an abusive relationship, and the fruit in your life will reflect that!

You were never designed to live a life of fear. God did not give you a spirit that shrinks when difficult situations come. He gave you a spirit that is mighty, self-controlled, and full of courageous love (2 Timothy 1:7). If you are struggling with fear, then you need to switch your mindset from the world's system to God's system. When you look to God's perfect love and His perfect promises, there is no fear.

Fear is best described by this commonly used acronym:

F: False
E: Evidence
A: Appearing
R: Real

Fear is perverted faith—it's faith in perverse things! It is when you trust in the world's system more than you trust in God's system. I've discovered that many people have faith that bad things will happen to them, but they aren't willing to have faith that good things can happen to them. Faith is the confidence that what we hope for will actually happen; it gives us assurance about things we cannot see (Hebrews 11:1).

Satan loves to present false evidence to you, and as long as you're operating in fear, you can't discern the truth. He knows how to push your buttons. He knows what to say to get you in fear. Since we have been brought up in a fear-driven culture, that's not hard for him either.

The Bible says that faith comes by hearing the Word of God, and if you put God's Word in your heart, then it will produce faith by itself (Romans 10:17). That principle works both ways. Fear comes by hearing and meditating on fearful situations. If you put stories in your heart that speak contrary to God's promises, then they will produce fear.

When false evidence attacks, what rises up in your spirit? How do you respond?

> *For the weapons of our warfare are not of the flesh, but divinely powerful for the destruction of fortresses. We are destroying speculations and every lofty thing raised up against the knowledge of God, and we are taking every thought captive to the obedience of Christ.*
> —2 Corinthians 10:4-5 (NASB 1995)

You were created to live in fearlessness, excitement, and freedom through God's love. You were created for that kind of perfect love where there is fearless abandonment. It comes from love, from spending time with God, and from setting aside the opinions of men and women.

Week 36: Break Up with Fear

Fear tries to make you its slave. But even when the emotion of fear comes on you, you don't have to obey it. You can speak to it and take authority over it. You can choose faith in God over fear and the world's system!

—Better Than You Think

Prayer Focus

Thank God that you can be courageous in every situation and move forward in the face of fear because He is always with you.

Think on It

→ What does the enemy try to use to bring fear into your life?

→ When was the last time you fought back against fear? What happened?

→ How do you think social media contributes to putting stories in your heart that speak contrary to God's promises?

Pursue Change

This week, be alert to how the enemy uses things to attempt to bring fear into your life or motivate you to take action because of fear. Consider taking a break from watching the news or scrolling through social media.

Meditate on Deuteronomy 31:6-8:

> *Be strong and courageous. Do not be afraid or terrified because of them, for the Lord your God goes with you; he will never leave you nor forsake you. Then Moses summoned Joshua and said to him in the presence of all Israel, "Be strong and courageous, for you must go with this people into the land that the Lord swore to their ancestors to give them, and you must divide it among them as their inheritance. The Lord himself goes before you and will be with you; he will never leave you nor forsake you. Do not be afraid; do not be discouraged."*

Notes

Week 37
Be Fully Persuaded

Week 37: Be Fully Persuaded

Now faith is the substance of things hoped for, the evidence of things not seen.

—Hebrews 11:1 (KJV)

"An evidence of faith is your ability to defend yourself in a spiritual court of law. Since faith is based on the Word of God, you must know why you believe what you believe."

— *Your Financial Revolution: The Power of Provision*

Let me give you an easy test you can give yourself to see if you are really in faith or not. Close your eyes, and what do you see?

Faith is the substance of things hoped for. Hope always carries a picture with it. If I promised you an ice cream cone, you would instantly have a picture of an ice cream cone in your mind. If you believed that I was honest in my offer and I had the means to pay for it, you would see yourself with that ice cream cone and be excited.

The same is true of the Word of God. When you believe a promise of God and are fully persuaded that God has the intent and the means to make good on His promise, you will see a picture of yourself with the promise. Even though you may not have the promised item at that very moment, you will act like you do, because in a sense you do. The promise is valid, the intent is valid, and it is yours. So faith, being fully persuaded of God's intent and power, is the substance of the promise to you. It is also the evidence of things yet unseen.

When you believe a promise of God and are fully persuaded that God has the intent and the means to make good on His promise, you will see a picture of yourself with the promise.

You still need to cash the check, which is a legal process that applies to the spiritual realm as it does in the natural world. So when I say, "Close your eyes. What do you see?"

Week 37: Be Fully Persuaded

what I am saying is this. If you can't see it, you can't seize it. Let me bring this down to a very simple statement. If you close your eyes and you do not see yourself with the promise, you are not in faith. If you are sick and when you close your eyes, you see yourself healed—I mean you see yourself healed as in no fear but instead with an absolute assurance that you are healed—that is faith. But if you close your eyes and still see yourself sick, waiting to be healed, then you are not in faith. If you need money and you believe a promise of God, then you are no longer anxious about money but you see yourself with the provision you need.

Fear Is the Opposite of Faith

Fear does not exist with this kind of confidence. If you are still nervous about the outcome, you are not in faith. In regard to faith, you need to know how to tell if you are in faith or not. You do not want to make major decisions if you are not in faith, because if you are not in faith, you are in fear. Fear always plays it safe and is unbelief. This is why I said to always sow your seed when you are in faith. You do not want to sow it as a formula, simply going through the motion of giving, because that will not produce anything. You want to be confident of what God says so that when you close your eyes, all you see is you and that promise. You already have it, you possess it, it is yours, and peace has replaced any anxiousness you may have had.

> *Do not be anxious about anything, but in every situation, by prayer and petition, with thanksgiving, present your requests to God. And the peace of God, which transcends all understanding, will guard your hearts and your minds in Christ Jesus.*
> —Philippians 4:6-7

When you are in faith, there is a peace that is not based on circumstances but on the promise.

Hold on to the Moment When You Released Your Faith

One thing that I remind people of is that there is always time between the "Amen" and the "There it is." Because of this, it is vital that you hold on to the moment of faith's release. I suggest that you write this down in your journal or on a note to remind yourself.

When circumstances tempt you to retreat in fear, you can remind yourself of the date and time you received your answer. Do not allow what may appear as a failure to lure you into letting go of your faith.

—*Your Financial Revolution: The Power of Provision*

Week 37: Be Fully Persuaded

Prayer Focus

Thank God that He is faithful, that He has a plan, and that He is never caught off guard or taken by surprise.

Think on It

→ When you close your eyes and think about your future, what do you see?

→ Are you fully persuaded that God has the intent and the means to make good on His promises to you?

→ Do you write down the moment you pray and release your faith about things? Why or why not? Will this change now?

Pursue Change

Take on a challenge this week. Print out an image of a fake blank check. Write it out to yourself. Put the word "ALL" in the amount box. Write "All of the promises" in the dollars blank, and sign it "GOD."

Of course, this isn't to pretend that you are God, or to cash a fake check, but to give you a visual that God has already given you His Kingdom—all of His precious promises. Hang or tape the check up somewhere where you will see it daily as a reminder that you already have everything you need.

Notes

Notes

Week 38

Turn Life's Negatives into Fuel

Week 38: Turn Life's Negatives into Fuel

A final word: Be strong in the Lord and in his mighty power. Put on all of God's armor so that you will be able to stand firm against all strategies of the devil.
—Ephesians 6:10-11 (NLT)

"Anytime you or I face difficulties in life, we must rewind and examine and challenge our experience against the Word of God, and let it shine light on the situation."

— *Better Than You Feel*

Every time we encounter a hardship or hurt in life, our human response is to store the memories, feelings, and emotions of that hurt and create a belief system about those situations. In almost every decision, we consult our existing belief system. If we believe the same experience will happen in the next attempt, we are programmed to stay in that mindset and actually create the same results. This can work for us if we have positive reinforcement, but if our experiences are negative or incite fear, we are set up for failure or we will retreat like a self-fulfilling prophecy.

We often build a wall of defense after hurtful experiences in order to protect ourselves from future similar encounters and to insulate ourselves from being hurt again. Our conclusions can be irrational and extreme or cause us to re-enter similar situations with expectations they will reoccur, and they almost always do when we believe so. Then wrong beliefs get a stronghold on our belief system. This is why it is imperative we renew our minds to God's Word and receive healing for our emotions. Allowing ourselves to feel better is part of this healing. Just because someone or something has hurt us in an area doesn't mean we should close ourselves off from attempting to do what God says we can do or have what He says we have in Christ Jesus.

This is particularly true in the area of love. Often, when someone has been through a painful marriage, they harden their heart and wall off their heart, believing that they could never experience joy in a long-lasting relationship. The

Week 38: Turn Life's Negatives into Fuel

enemy is all too quick to oblige their pain by substituting counterfeit plans or pursuits. Unresolved hurt can turn into fear and paralyze people from being able to move forward. The answer to this is to renew our minds to what God says about the situation and to forgive ourselves and others who have inflicted wounds or made poor decisions. Everyone makes mistakes, and the only perfect example is Jesus.

Analyze what went wrong, let the Word of God be your guidepost, and separate your belief system from the actual event. Just because your marriage was painful doesn't mean all marriages must be painful and, therefore, marriage is to be avoided at all costs. To believe all marriages will be dysfunctional would be adopting a wrong belief system based on feelings, not facts. That is not scriptural or rational. Just because you encountered bankruptcy doesn't mean that you are doomed to repeat it again. Just because slavery existed in the past doesn't mean that every person of a different race is a bigot and out to take advantage of other ethnicities. Just because a family member died of a certain disease doesn't mean you will.

Irrational fears and painful memories can hold us captive in a prison of "defeat and repeat" and cause us to disconnect from the possibility of a great future.

No matter what we endeavor to do or have, whether it is love or financial success, both come with challenges and require a price. When difficulties arise, if you haven't made up your mind and will that you can do all things through Christ, trials and self-defeating feelings will kick in. Quitting is the natural response, but it is rarely the best one. Any worthwhile endeavor will take an all-out commitment and a fight for the promises of God's Word. Spiritual warfare is a reality, and we can sell ourselves short by thinking that success will come easily without a fight.

Too often, people assume if God is in something, it will be effortless. On the contrary, we have an adversarial force trying to stop us from following God's plan. If our mental and emotional responses agree with the problem instead of with God's Word, we will not have the force to create answers to combat the problem. We must be convinced that there is an answer and we can win. Pressure seems to consistently be at its greatest before a breakthrough, like drilling through a hard surface. The heat intensifies in the thick of it. The saying, "It's always darkest before the dawn" definitely has merit.

We can develop peace and joy in the storms, but there are thunderclouds we encounter in all endeavors to build our lives. We must develop and grow spiritual muscle, by exercise, to respond differently. When we respond with faith in God's Word, storms must calm and mountains must move.

—Better Than You Feel

Week 38: Turn Life's Negatives into Fuel

Prayer Focus

Thank God that He has put everything under our dominion (Hebrews 2:7) and that His Word says if we submit to Him and resist the devil, the devil will flee from us (James 4:7).

Think on It

→ Have you ever assumed that if God was in something, it would be effortless?

→ Can you think of a time in your life when the pressure seemed to be at its greatest just before you experienced a breakthrough?

→ What do you do on a regular basis to build your "spiritual muscles"?

Pursue Change

This week, think about whether or not you have retreated from anything God has called you to do because of pressure. If so, begin to renew your mind to the Word of God. Learn what the Word says, and stay in agreement with what God says. Cast aside thoughts that are coming at you that don't line up with the Word, and be courageous enough to wade into the face of circumstances—into the pressure—and declare the Word over situations.

Notes

Notes

Week 39

Give Your Tithe in Faith

"Bring all the tithes into the storehouse, that there may be food in My house, and try Me now in this," says the Lord of hosts, "If I will not open for you the windows of heaven and pour out for you such blessing that there will not be room enough to receive it. And I will rebuke the devourer for your sakes, so that he will not destroy the fruit of your ground, nor shall the vine fail to bear fruit for you in the field," says the Lord of hosts; "and all nations will call you blessed, for you will be a delightful land," says the Lord of hosts.

—Malachi 3:10-12 (NKJV)

"The law of the tithe has not passed away. But the legal requirement to tithe has. Now, we have the choice to tithe and take advantage of its benefits."

— *Your Financial Revolution: The Power of Generosity*

Today, there is much confusion in the body of Christ around the tithe, what it is, and whether it is still in effect or passed away with the coming of Jesus. As you've probably heard me say, when God told me to learn all I could about how His Kingdom operated, I really became a spiritual scientist. I wanted to know how everything worked, and the tithe was a big question that I had to answer. So let's take a look at the tithe, where it came from, what it does, and why it is for today.

The tithe was started clear back in the beginning and gives God legal jurisdiction to step in between the devourer, Satan, and God's people and to rebuke Satan.

See, when Adam fell, Satan would have just loved to completely starve him off the planet. But immediately, God put the tithe in place to protect Adam and Eve. When Adam and Eve chose to tithe, they were putting God first. They were choosing God.

Let's remember that Satan gained his entrance into the earth realm in the same manner. By convincing Adam and Eve to believe him instead of God, he gained legal entrance. So by tithing—giving God 10% of what they had—it gave God the legal right to protect Adam and Eve's provision.

We need to remember that the tithe was a law that pertained only to man's provision on the earth in Satan's territory. It did not change their status in regard to bringing

Week 39: Give Your Tithe in Faith

spiritual restoration. No, a sacrifice for sin would have to be made first before that could happen. But the tithe did allow God to stop Satan from stealing provision from them, and it would allow them to survive on the earth.

Many people say that the tithe was an Old Testament law and has now passed away, having been fulfilled by Jesus's sacrifice. But we have seen that the law of the tithe was put in place clear back at the fall of man before the Law of Moses was written.

The tithe was put in place to act as a legal fence around Adam and Eve then, and it still acts as a legal shield around us today.

The tithe is a law of the earth realm and remains in force as long as Satan is loose on the earth, as he currently is. As long as Satan is here, the law of the tithe is still in effect.

Another thing you may see in church are people who are tithing and yet not prospering. This is because of some wrong teaching in regard to the tithe. People think if they just tithe, the blessing of the Lord will cause them to enjoy overflowing prosperity, more than they could contain. When they begin to tithe but do not see their prosperity overflowing, they conclude that the tithe does not work. But their assumption is not accurate.

God told the people that if they tithed, "*I will prevent pests from devouring your crops, and the vines in your fields will not drop their fruit before it is ripe"* (Malachi 3:11, NIV).

The Scripture says that the windows of heaven will be opened and God will bless their crops. The point I am making is that you still have to grow something inside the fence of the tithe.

The tithe by itself does not cause you to prosper. It only protects what you do inside of the fence, the tithe.

It is what you build or grow inside the fence that causes you to overflow with abundance.

Sadly, with wrong teaching, many of God's people tithe and then sit down with an iced tea and wait for the abundant overflow to begin. The overflow will begin when we understand our part in the process.

—Your Financial Revolution: The Power of Generosity

Week 39: Give Your Tithe in Faith

Prayer Focus

Thank God for the benefits and blessings of the tithe. Ask Him to give you a heart to always see the tithe as what it truly is, worship.

Think on It

→ Do you believe God's Kingdom won't survive without your money?

→ What incorrect things have you been taught about the tithe?

→ Has this book excerpt about the tithe changed your thinking? If so, how?

Pursue Change

The tithe allows God to step in. When you voluntarily give the first and the best of your money—your provision—to God, you give Him legal access to your money and your finances. It sanctifies, and separates, and stops Satan from being able to steal, kill, or destroy your financial life. The tithe sets a fence; it rebukes the devourer; it stops the legal dominion Satan has to steal, kill, and destroy.

Of course, just because you have a fence doesn't mean that anything inside it grows by itself. That's where offerings come in. Putting tithes and offerings into place allows God to bless the work of your hands.

God says, "Test me in this!" Do you hear His heart in that? He's saying, "Let Me show you how much I love you! Let Me show you how I want to bless you!"

If you haven't been tithing or giving offerings, this is the week to change that.

Notes

Week 40

Make Every Effort to Live in Peace

Make every effort to live in peace with everyone and to be holy; without holiness no one will see the Lord. See to it that no one falls short of the grace of God and that no bitter root grows up to cause trouble and defile many.

—Hebrews 12:14-15

"No matter what you're dealing with in your marriage today, don't forget that your spouse isn't the enemy. Stand on the Word of God, and speak it into your situation."

— *Nasty Gets Us Nowhere*

So many couples talk about how hard marriage is, but marriage isn't the issue. Marriage only reveals what's already inside of us. The real issue is our desire to do things our way, when and how we want. Marriage is God's plan to help us see ourselves in the mirror of how we treat others. Without it, we tend to just become more self-centered and demanding, which ultimately shows up in every relationship. You can see this so clearly in our culture. We need strong marriages and homes again to save America and the world from self-destruction. Children need the security and love that strong marriages bring.

When I look back at the beginning of my marriage, I know it wasn't hard—we were.

STRATEGIES TO RESOLVE CONFLICT

Here are four powerful strategies to resolve conflict in your marriage and walk in unity with your spouse. These can also be helpful in any other relationship.

1. PUT YOURSELF IN THEIR SHOES.

> Selfishness asks, "How will this affect *me*?" Love asks, "How will this affect *them*?"

> When we learned to understand where the other person was coming from, our communication improved.

Week 40: Make Every Effort to Live in Peace

2. KNOW WHEN TO LET THINGS GO.

> Satan is after the power of agreement because strife opens the door to him. When Gary and I were tempted to argue in the early years of our marriage, we would look at each other and say, "I'd rather prosper." It was immature, but it was our cue to let things go instead of arguing.
>
> Sometimes, our greatest strength in dealing with conflict is knowing when to back down, walk it off, or take a breather. Ask yourself, "Is this really something worth fighting over? Will I care about this situation a year from now?"
>
> When strife tries to enter the scene, know when you need to walk it off or take a breather before you say something you can't take back. We have to remember we aren't trying to win the conversation; we are simply trying to come to an agreement. That often means we must learn to meet in the middle.

3. DIVORCE OR WALKING AWAY ISN'T AN OPTION.

> Divorce, walking away from a friendship, or refusing to be on a project with a coworker should never be an option. Gary and I have never talked about divorce or even thought about it. For us, it's not a possibility. When you use divorce as a power play in heated

conversations with your spouse, you compromise the foundation of your relationship.

A healthy marriage should be a safe place where we can talk through issues without worrying about the other person threatening to walk out the door. Bringing up the idea of divorce in arguments will make both you and your spouse feel insecure and unsafe in your relationship. It often puts a hurdle between spouses that is difficult to remove even after the heat of the moment is gone.

4. PRAY TOGETHER AND FOR EACH OTHER.

Prayer only takes a few seconds, but it has the power to change the very course of our future. It's our superpower in faith, but it is one of the easiest things to put on the back burner in our day.

The moments when we should pray the most are often the times when we pray the least, such as when we're struggling to communicate with our spouse. In those moments when we're angry, upset, and tired of trying to talk to each other, often the last thing we think about is praying for the other person. We don't want to talk to them, let alone pray for them.

Prayer has the power to change atmospheres, hearts, and minds. When we're having a conflict with our

Week 40: Make Every Effort to Live in Peace

spouse, that's when we need prayer the most.

As a husband and wife, you have to come to the place of unity. It may take some time and some work, but it's worth it. Changes in your family are going to start from the head down—from you and your husband, from your marriage, and then to your children and family. Praying *for* your spouse is one of the most important habits you can cultivate in your day. Praying *with* your spouse is one of the most important habits you can cultivate in your life.

So let me ask you: How is your prayer life right now? Are you praying for your spouse daily? Are you praying with your spouse daily? I encourage you to release God's power and love into your marriage. Trust God and turn your situation over to Him.

—*Nasty Gets Us Nowhere*

Prayer Focus

Ask God to help you show empathy and understanding, to recognize the power of prayer in your relationships, and to know when to let go. Thank Him in advance for helping you have a peaceful resolution to every conflict.

Think on It

→ How would you describe a "peaceful" relationship?

→ When was the last time you saw something from someone else's perspective? What happened?

→ How do you go about "choosing your battles" in life?

Pursue Change

This week, take time to actually do the four powerful strategies for resolving conflict listed in this week's book excerpt with someone who you tend to have conflict with and see what happens. Pray and ask God to show you how you can help better the relationship and improve communication.

Notes

Week 41
Have More Than Enough

Week 41: Have More Than Enough

The Lord will grant you abundant prosperity—in the fruit of your womb, the young of your livestock and the crops of your ground—in the land he swore to your ancestors to give you.

The Lord will open the heavens, the storehouse of his bounty, to send rain on your land in season and to bless all the work of your hands. You will lend to many nations but will borrow from none. The Lord will make you the head, not the tail. If you pay attention to the commands of the Lord your God that I give you this day and carefully follow them, you will always be at the top, never at the bottom.

—Deuteronomy 28:11-13

> "Without the proper picture, knowing what our lives are supposed to be like, we will fall for the tricks and traps and the perverted thinking of the earth curse system. Faith is staying in agreement with what God says, not with our circumstances."
>
> — *Your Financial Revolution: The Power of Rest*

By now, you know that this Sabbath rest is a promise to every New Testament believer in Christ, and it is not just an Old Testament thing. You also know now that the Sabbath is not possible without having more than enough, or as we saw in Exodus 16, the double portion. Please do not confuse walking in the double portion to mean that you will in every case have a huge cash surplus on hand when God asks you to move on a project.

There have been times in my life when Jesus told me to move forward on a project when I did not have any of the money in the bank. I realized later that God was never nervous about the money and knew where it would come from. But He did not allow it to manifest lest the enemy try to steal it before it was actually needed. Let me caution you: Only make a

Week 41: Have More Than Enough

decision to move forward in a situation like that if you are sure you have heard from the Holy Spirit to do so. Again, unless Jesus tells you to move forward on a project without the funds in place, do not move forward on it. Wait for the timing of God, and the provision to be available.

In general, we as believers are called to live out of the financial overflow of our lives. We are not paupers but are able to be generous on every occasion just as our Father is. I only mention that because I have received so many emails where people jumped out there and missed God's timing. Listen, just because God shows you something does not mean it is time to move on it. Many times, He shows you something to give you direction and time for preparation. In my experience, timing is just as important as hearing direction in the first place.

When Jesus began His ministry in His hometown, after He had been baptized in the Jordan River by John the Baptist and after the 40 days and nights in the wilderness, He went into His local synagogue and picked up the scroll of Isaiah and turned to the sixty-first chapter and read.

> *The Spirit of the Sovereign Lord is on me, because the Lord has anointed me to proclaim good news to the poor. He has sent me to bind up the brokenhearted, to proclaim freedom for the captives and release from darkness for the prisoners, to proclaim the year of the Lord's favor and the day of vengeance of our*

> *God, to comfort all who mourn.*
>
> —Isaiah 61:1-2

When He had finished reading, He handed the scroll back to the attendants and said, "Today this Scripture has been fulfilled in your hearing." Of course, they were furious at Him for implying that He was the one it was referring to. Jesus had read just the first couple of verses of Isaiah 61 as He was making a declaration of who He was, but the entire chapter applies to us, the New Testament church. In regard to the double portion, take a look at verses seven through nine.

> *Instead of your shame you will receive a double portion, and instead of disgrace you will rejoice in your inheritance; and so you will inherit a double portion in your land, and everlasting joy will be yours. For I, the Lord, love justice; I hate robbery and wrongdoing. In my faithfulness I will reward my people and make an everlasting covenant with them. Their descendants will be known among the nations and their offspring among the peoples. All who see them will acknowledge that they are a people the Lord has blessed.*
>
> —Isaiah 61:7-9

The double portion is yours, Jesus is your Sabbath rest, and He is your double portion!

—*Your Financial Revolution: The Power of Rest*

Week 41: Have More Than Enough

Prayer Focus

Thank God for designing creation so that you can live and exist in the seventh day with Him and without worry for your provision. Thank Him that you have the ability to gather and produce wealth supernaturally.

Think on It

→ Are you currently able to be generous on every occasion?

→ Have you ever prematurely moved on something God told you to do?

→ Do you believe God wants you to have money?

Pursue Change

The ability to gather and produce the double portion happens through God-given ideas, direction, and timing. As you listen to God, He will direct you to harvest ideas and concepts that you were not aware of previously. It's this flow of ideas and new concepts that God will use to revolutionize your life.

This week, keep a prayer journal and list all of the new ideas that come to you in prayer and throughout the day.

Notes

Notes

Week 42
Walk in Confidence

Finally, brothers and sisters, whatever is true, whatever is noble, whatever is right, whatever is pure, whatever is lovely, whatever is admirable—if anything is excellent or praiseworthy—think about such things.

—Philippians 4:8

"When negative thoughts start to rise up in you, challenge them with the Word of God."

— *Shark Proof*

> *"You wouldn't worry so much about what others think of you if you realized how seldom they do."*
> —Eleanor Roosevelt

Insecurity.

It's the silent voice that tries to tell us what to do, what to think, and how to feel about ourselves and the people we love. Insecurity is the wave that we ride into the jaws of sharks. Unchecked, it becomes a PRISON around us... It often makes us more susceptible to shark wounds, keeps us paralyzed in unhealthy situations, and worse yet, makes us want to get out of the water for good.

Insecurities can haunt us!

- *Do people think I'm weird?*
- *Am I lovable?*
- *Am I capable?*
- *Do I need to lose weight?*
- *Have I made too many mistakes?*
- *Can I really do this?*
- *Am I pretty enough?*
- *Am I a failure?*

Tormenting thoughts begin to swell in our minds, and we can become paralyzed in the water beneath the pressure. Our perception of reality can actually be changed by these thoughts!

Week 42: Walk in Confidence

When I was a young woman, I struggled with perfectionism; occasionally I still do. I wanted to be perfect—hair, clothing, shoes, makeup. I didn't realize at the time that my insecurity was derailing my God-given purpose. My worth was wrapped up in other people's opinions. If I was perfect, I thought people would accept me, people would love me. It wasn't true. People can't give you what you don't have, and they can't give you what they don't have.

When you don't know who you are in Christ, you feel insecure, but when your identity is firm in Christ, you are free to be who you are, who God made you to be.

When you learn who you are, you trade perfectionism for enthusiasm—enthusiasm for relationships, for life, for your God-designed dreams, and, most importantly, for joy and laughter!

When we tolerate insecurities, we start bouncing our identities off of the people and media around us, looking for something to confirm or deny our inner fears…

Did anyone compliment my outfit today? Am I as pretty as that movie star? Did she say she was busy because she didn't want to hang out with me?

We become shark bait!

And the worst part is Satan will put people, media, and situations in our lives to discourage us and feed those insecurities.

> *"The reason why we struggle with insecurity is because we compare our behind-the-scenes with everyone else's highlight reel."*
>
> —Steven Furtick

Insecurities can cause us to:

- Endure hurtful or unhealthy relationships
- Lash out at the people around us
- Use manipulation to get attention and affirmation
- Become easily offended and overreact to situations
- Battle depression, fear, and hopelessness
- Withdraw from the people we love
- Beat ourselves up over small mistakes
- Give up on ourselves
- Become possessive of the people we love

> *"If you set out to be liked, you would be prepared to compromise on anything at any time, and you would achieve nothing."*
>
> —Margaret Thatcher

My friend, insecurities will either make you shark bait or a shark!

If we tolerate insecurity, it's like a weed that chokes out our hope, happiness, and trust in the people around us.
When we water insecurity, it grows!

Week 42: Walk in Confidence

When Insecurity Knocks

So what do you do when insecurity comes knocking at your door?

How do you shut down the seeds of self-doubt before they blossom into paralyzing uncertainty?

So first, we're instructed to PRAY. If we feel insecurity beginning to grab ahold of us, we need to turn to God and ask Him for His help in the situation. We need to pray for the grace to walk in confidence.

The second thing we're called to do is to change what we're LOOKING at!

If you are battling an insecurity, you need to adamantly shut down the voices and images speaking that into your life. If you feel bad about your body or looks, stop spending hours browsing through photos of Instagram models and movie stars in tabloid magazines. Start putting your focus on things that are going to encourage you instead!

Did you know that God put everything in you that you need for your destiny? With Him, you are lacking nothing and are able to do impossible things!

Psalm 139:14 says, *"I praise you because I am fearfully and wonderfully made; your works are wonderful, I know that full well."*

—*Shark Proof*

Prayer Focus

Praise God that you are fearfully and wonderfully made by Him (Psalm 139:14). Ask Him to give you His grace to continually walk in the confidence that you are fully known (Psalm 139) and deeply loved by Him.

Think on It

→ In what area(s) of your life are you most likely to battle insecurity? Why?

→ Has insecurity ever kept you from doing something you know God was leading you to do? What happened?

→ Which of the things on the list in this week's book excerpt does insecurity most often cause you to do (endure hurtful or unhealthy relationships, lash out at the people around you, etc.)?

Week 42: Walk in Confidence

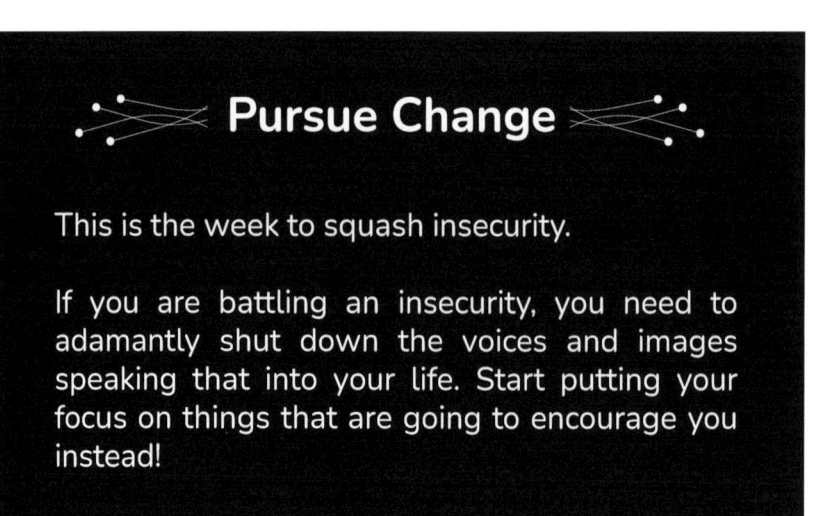

Pursue Change

This is the week to squash insecurity.

If you are battling an insecurity, you need to adamantly shut down the voices and images speaking that into your life. Start putting your focus on things that are going to encourage you instead!

Notes

Week 43

Enjoy the Kingdom of God

"By knowing exactly what your legal rights are as a citizen of heaven, knowing what has already been freely given to you, understanding the process to receive, and enjoying the benefit of those laws, you can walk in a whole new way of living—the Kingdom way."

— *Your Financial Revolution: The Power of Allegiance*

If you knew without a shadow of a doubt that prayer is effective and all of heaven backs it up, would that make you confident when you pray? YES!!!

What would happen to fear? What would happen to uncertainty? How would that knowledge prompt confidence toward your future and confidence in the midst of a storm?

This was the impact the Kingdom had on Drenda and me when we began to discover it. We were constantly surprised and amazed! Even more so, we were amazed at the authority that God has given to the church to operate on behalf of and through that government here in the earth realm.

To find out that we were freed from the "law of sin and death" and given the Kingdom and access to the "law of the Spirit of life" was overwhelming. Again, more overwhelming to us was actually watching that law produce the righteousness of the Kingdom in our very lives.

Drenda and I were so excited that we would tell anyone who would listen about the Kingdom and tell them our story. People in our church were catching on and having the same results we were, and one of those people was our own 12-year-old daughter. She had seen God do so much and had witnessed time and time again the unfailing

Week 43: Enjoy the Kingdom of God

laws of the Kingdom produce in our lives. I knew she was watching and learning about these laws, but one story showed me just how much she was indeed learning.

One day I went up to her bedroom to say good night, and something was different. There on her wall was a picture of a Pomeranian dog. Now, for any parent who has been around a bit, such a picture is a sure sign that they are about to be asked for a dog. Well, I decided to head this off at the pass as I did not want another indoor dog.

I thought the matter was finished until one day about a month later when we got home from church. Kirsten walked confidently up to me and, with a smile on her face, said, "Dad, today I received a Pomeranian puppy by faith just like you teach." I reminded her again of my previous statements about not having another dog. Without changing her smile, she stated, "But, Dad, Mom says that God can change the heart of a king." Her comment to me was not rebellious. She simply agreed with her mother and prayed that God would change my heart. I was had. I now knew that her mother and she had talked, and her mother had encouraged her that God could indeed change my mind.

Based on that encouragement, she had released her faith that morning in church, sowed, and confessed she had received that dog by faith. I dug my heels in and reassured her of my love and again stated my case and told her, "We are not going to have another dog in the house." I said that

I was sorry, but it just was not going to happen. She did not seem to care what I said; she walked away smiling.

About a month later, I was invited to teach at a small church in Mississippi. It was a very small country church surrounded by miles of open land. At the end of the first night, the pastor walked up to me and said the Lord had spoken to him during the service. He said, "I do not know if you know this or not, but I raise Pomeranians on the side, and the Lord told me to give you one of the puppies that are now six weeks old and ready to find a home." I stood there with my mouth hanging open.

How did that dog show up? I had never had a dog offered to me before. And how was it the specific dog that my daughter had released her faith for? Was it a fluke? No, obviously not. It was a direct result of the Kingdom and the laws that govern it producing in my family's life. They produced just like they will every time for anyone who has faith and releases Kingdom authority here in the earth realm.

—Your Financial Revolution: The Power of Allegiance

Week 43: Enjoy the Kingdom of God

Prayer Focus

Thank God that He has already given you the WHOLE Kingdom to enjoy. Tell Him how excited you are to see the Kingdom impact every area of your life, even the small nonessential areas.

Think on It

→ Do you go around telling anyone who will listen about the Kingdom of God?

→ Is there something you would like to have show up in your life like the Pomeranian puppy did for our daughter?

→ Do you think there is anything too small or unimportant to bring under the dominion of the Kingdom? If so, give an example.

Pursue Change

This week, meditate on Mark 11:24:

THEREFORE I TELL YOU, WHATEVER YOU ASK FOR IN PRAYER, BELIEVE THAT YOU HAVE RECEIVED IT, AND IT WILL BE YOURS.

Notice that it says "WHATEVER," not "when you ask about the big things in prayer, believe that you have received it." No, we worship a God who cares about every aspect of our lives. Talk to Him like the friend that He is and ask Him for what you have need of.

Notes

Notes

Week 44
Clean Out the Junk

Week 44: Clean Out the Junk

And you will know the truth, and the truth will set you free.

—John 8:32 (NLT)

"Clean out those self-destructive mindsets and bad habits that are dooming you to failure!"

— *Better Than You Think*

The mind loves to be right. If you think you're a failure, then your mind is going to give you a pretty convincing argument. Sometimes you have to tell your mind to be quiet and to listen to your spirit.

It is easy to hold onto the words people have said about us, the times people have sinned against us, and our previous shortcomings and insecurity. Sometimes we don't even realize we are allowing toxic mindsets to control us!

When Gary and I were newlyweds, I imagined these elaborate, romantic scenarios I wanted. I'd suggest we go on a date, and I would spend that week thinking about how I wanted it to go—the romantic things he would say, the flowers he would surprise me with, and I would picture it like it was something out of a romantic comedy.

Then the date would come. Gary wouldn't say what I had scripted for him in my mind. My hair wouldn't look the way I wanted. I couldn't find anything perfect to wear. I would let a bunch of small things ruin my night! Instead of enjoying those moments for what they were, and realizing the great thing I had, I would get offended with Gary for something he didn't even do. It was so silly! How could he know what I wanted him to say anyway?

That is how toxic mindsets work though. They stop you from enjoying life by moving your thoughts from the good things God is doing and the blessing right in front of you

Week 44: Clean Out the Junk

and instead focusing them on toxic lies. And in the end, you're the one who misses out on what God has for you.

Do you need to forgive someone? Are you rehearsing a hurt that you've been through? Are you talking the hurt instead of talking the promise?

It does not matter who got you where you are; what matters is where you are going from here. If God has forgiven you (which He has), you need to choose forgiveness for someone else. You may have had unmet expectations of a person or even of God, but God wants to heal those damaged areas inside of you.

It's not over. God's not finished doing a work in you. Just because you don't see the answer yet doesn't mean it's not coming.

> *You need to persevere so that when you have done the will of God, you will receive what He has promised.*
> —Hebrews 10:36

Don't quit! We've been through tough times, but tough times don't last. The Word of God and the promises of God are eternal. They are always there!

The Bible says that Jesus is the same yesterday, today, forever, and He's no respecter of persons (Hebrews 13:8,

Acts 10:34). What He did for Gary and Drenda Keesee, He will do for you. What He promises to any of us is a promise for all of us. You have to believe it. If you don't believe it, you can't receive it. You can't allow past experiences to cause you to develop the wrong pattern of thinking.

If your mind is renewed to toxic thoughts, you are carrying around a big, red self-destruct button. You can't move forward until you decide to think like God thinks and throw out your toxic thoughts.

What is your reality?

Identify the toxic thoughts that could potentially lead you to self-destruction. Write them down. Start with who people told you that you were or who you should be. We often carry those negative labels from our past with us every day, projecting our past hurts onto our future possibilities.

Identity is a huge stumbling point for many. If you feel unworthy, guilty, ugly, incompetent, insecure, anxious, unlovable, or weak, write those toxic mindsets down. And don't forget mindsets like wishing you could change your body or that habit of running to the refrigerator when you're stressed or bored. Anything that does not line up with God's Word, whether it is big or small, has to go!

—*Better Than You Think*

Week 44: Clean Out the Junk

Prayer Focus

Praise God that Jesus is the same yesterday, today, forever, and He's no respecter of persons (Hebrews 13:8, Acts 10:34). Thank Him that He hasn't finished doing a work in you.

Think on It

→ Do you have trouble admitting when you're wrong?

→ Do you have more of a tendency to focus on the positive or on the negative? Why?

→ Do you need to forgive someone? What's stopping you?

Pursue Change

It's time to throw out toxic thoughts and start thinking like God thinks.

This week, work on identifying the toxic thoughts that could potentially lead you to self-destruction. Write them down. Start with who people told you that you were or who you should be. We often carry those negative labels from our past with us every day and project our past hurts onto our future possibilities.

Identity is a huge stumbling point for many. If you feel unworthy, guilty, ugly, incompetent, insecure, anxious, unlovable, or weak, write those toxic mindsets down. And don't forget mindsets like wishing you could change your body or that habit of running to the refrigerator when you're stressed or bored. Anything that does not line up with God's Word, whether it is big or small, has to go!

Notes

Week 45

Take Time to Prepare

No, we declare God's wisdom, a mystery that has been hidden and that God destined for our glory before time began. None of the rulers of this age understood it, for if they had, they would not have crucified the Lord of glory.

—1 Corinthians 2:7-8

"Why is the Kingdom of God compared to a treasure? Because if you have access to heaven's knowledge, you can know what to do in every situation with unique and unusual God-given strategies."

— *Your Financial Revolution: The Power of Strategy*

I always say that God's secrets are hidden *for* you, not *from* you! Satan dwells in darkness and does not know the plans of God. He can only react to what God is doing. By the time he finds out what is going on, it is too late! So the next time you get a little nervous as the midnight hour approaches and you still do not have your answer, know that God is never late, and what you may see as a delay is working for you by keeping the answer hidden until it is time for it to be revealed.

> *The kingdom of heaven is like treasure HIDDEN in a field. When a man found it, he hid it again, and then in his joy went and sold all he had and bought that field.*
>
> —Matthew 13:44

We have discussed what and where the field is and why the treasure is hidden. We have also discussed how to hear those hidden things from the Kingdom of God by praying in the Spirit and listening for the Holy Spirit's voice. But there is another vital principle in this process listed in our Scripture that you must know. Not heeding it has caused the downfall of many good and noble plans and caused devastating destruction in people's lives.

Notice in our Scripture that once the man hears the treasure, the idea, the direction, or the plan from God, it says he hides it again. HE DOES NOT ACT ON IT right away! He does not start telling all of his friends and neighbors about what he

Week 45: Take Time to Prepare

has heard from the Lord or of his new and exciting plans, not yet anyway. The Bible says that he hides it again, goes and sells all he has, and then buys the field. In simple terms, he does not want to reveal the location of the treasure to anyone else until he actually owns it. By waiting until he owns it, he is assured that no one can steal it from him.

The Scripture also reveals that at the time he first finds the treasure, he is not actually in a position to pay for the treasure and must go through a process of preparation to enable him to purchase it. This principle goes far beyond money and simply buying something. It is teaching us a vital principle of life and how you are to act on what the Holy Spirit shows you if you want to succeed.

The Scripture is saying that once you hear the idea or direction, you must not move on it until you have the capacity to occupy it. I think we can all easily see how this works with money. If you do not have enough money to buy the land, you certainly would not tell someone that there was a treasure on it. If word got out that there was a treasure on it, you can be sure that someone else would buy it first. Instead, you would go and do whatever it took to get the money to purchase the land, all the while keeping the truth about the hidden treasure to yourself.

This same principle is true for every direction or instruction that God may give you. Many times, Christians miss the beginning for the end. Many times, the Holy Spirit will reveal an idea to us, not revealing it for us to move on the idea at that moment but to allow us to prepare so that we can actually capture the opportunity. The preparation phase of any endeavor is the most important part of the process. In sports, games are lost or won based on how well the teams prepare for the game during practice, when no one is watching.

When we hear an idea from the Holy Spirit, it does not mean we are to jump out at that moment. Most of the time, it is leading us to hide that dream and prepare to occupy it. Usually, we do not have all we need to occupy that vision with success. Preparation may take a week or even years depending on what God has shown you to do. You must understand that preparation and timing are just as important or more important than the idea itself!

—Your Financial Revolution: The Power of Strategy

Week 45: Take Time to Prepare

Prayer Focus

Thank God for the unusual ways He is advancing His Kingdom right under the nose of the enemy. Ask Him to help you keep your spiritual ears and eyes open and your heart obedient so that you can avoid the enemy and advance in life.

Think on It

→ Do you have trouble patiently waiting for all God has for you?

→ Have you ever started something without properly preparing? What happened?

→ What do you believe God is doing in you now to prepare you for what He has next for you?

Pursue Change

You must have spiritual ears to hear God's strategy for your life. Now is the time to train yourself to discern these things.

This week, start practicing. Take the time to understand the mysteries of the Kingdom that God reveals so you can stand your ground and really build something. To many people, the Bible is just stories, but when you're born again, it's full of revelation. Ask God to reveal the mysteries and you'll see that the next time you study, you'll say, "Wait a minute! Has that really been there all along?" He'll give you a glimpse of your destiny. If you will have ears to hear, submit, and walk it out, you're going to have an incredible story.

Notes

Notes

Week 46

Be Teachable

Week 46: Be Teachable

"If you were blind, you wouldn't be guilty," Jesus replied. "But you remain guilty because you claim you can see."
—John 9:41 (NLT)

"Ultimately, we must trust God, open our hearts to the Holy Spirit, and cling to God's Word and love over all other voices or responses. Offenses are the tactics Satan uses to get us to close down, oftentimes to our own answer."
— *Better Than You Feel*

Satan knows how to play on our emotions, which sets us up for conflicts in our soul and offenses with others that can end in separation and division. He baits us with offenses to divide and conquer. It is not flesh and blood that you wrestle with but powers, principalities, might, dominion, and everything that sets itself up against the knowledge of God's Word (Ephesians 6:12). We must wake up to his tactics and stop being tossed around like children who are naïve and easily tricked by bad guys. This requires emotional maturity developed by training in God's Word, and it requires humility and our choice to be teachable.

Too many times, people blame God for hardships in their lives when, oftentimes, it is the work of their own hearts that create their problems. Offenses or holding grudges, which are forms of unforgiveness, account for calloused hearts and lead us to betray. We have all been betrayed, and we have all betrayed someone.

We all have tendencies to find fault in others and to use those faults to justify our own wrongdoing, but this doesn't fly with God. Just like the Israelites circled through the wilderness for years when God had promised them a land of abundance, many believers are wandering around disconnected from God's leadership, blessings, and provision because of offenses and wounds. Ministers have left their posts, and disciples have stopped their support of leadership. This tactic of Satan to divide and conquer has greatly damaged hearts and ministries. It's time to reconcile

Week 46: Be Teachable

differences and see the big picture, which is more important than foolish arguments that create strife. It's time to come into a place of maturity in Christ and the abundance that comes with obedience.

Pride: The Ultimate Blinder

Pride is the protector of all evil in our hearts and lives. When we can humbly admit we were wrong, we can change and bring change. "*If my people, who are called by name, will humble themselves and pray… I will heal their land*" (2 Chronicles 7:14). Why are we afraid to admit we are wrong and afraid to receive healing? Wounded emotions.

When we are mistreated or experience injustice, we have two choices: to forgive and let God take our case or to retain the offense and take up our own case with a personal vengeance to get even. One requires humility, and the other is based in stubborn pride. Pride causes us to literally fall over. It's like stumbling over our own feet. Pride becomes the guard at the gate of our heart, and wounded emotions are on the inside. Those wounds need to be healed so we can receive all that God has, but if we keep pride guarding the door to our heart, how can God's healing get in?

Throughout years of providing counsel and pastoral leadership, I've witnessed people harm themselves and their families to protect their pride. God can give grace to humble people, but He casts out a proud person. Why? You can't teach a proud person anything. They think they are right and will fight to prove it and to prove you wrong. They may think they've won the battle, but in the long run, they lose the war. They're the only ones who can't see it, even though it becomes evident to those around them and impacts business negotiations, finances, spiritual growth, and relationships.

When Dealing with Offenses:

1. Talk to the person you have an issue with about the person or situation and not to others. If you have an issue or fault with your brother, GO TO HIM, not around him.

2. Don't take up others' offenses and become a third party in the middle of a concern or conflict. Third parties lose. Rightfully, the Scripture says to mind your own business and lead a peaceable life. (See 1 Thessalonians 4:11.) There is no peace when you try to take false responsibility for situations that don't involve you.

3. Don't stuff feelings down inside unless you want them to explode when you least expect it.

Maturity in our emotions and fruitfulness happen when we can admit our failings, receive counsel, and hold our actions to the standard of God's Word rather than justifying ourselves and blaming others.

—*Better Than You Feel*

Week 46: Be Teachable

Prayer Focus

Ask God to give you patience and to help you always overlook offenses (Proverbs 19:11).

Think on It

> Do you consider yourself to be teachable? Why or why not?

> How often do you find yourself trying to protect your pride?

> How do you normally handle an offense? Does it need to change?

Pursue Change

This week, make sure that your ways mirror the Word of God so you can live free and inherit the blessings of God for your life. While you should absolutely not compromise truth to keep from getting your feelings hurt, you also shouldn't be on a mission to blast people with offensive actions or attitudes. Check yourself and make sure you're representing God well.

Notes

Notes

Week 47
Look for Opportunities

Week 47: Look for Opportunities

This is what the Lord says to you: "Do not be afraid or discouraged because of this vast army. For the battle is not yours, but God's."

—2 Chronicles 20:15b

"People pay big money to clean up or fix problems. A business is really an answer to someone's problem."

— *Your Financial Revolution: The Power of Provision*

People tell me that when they stepped out, all hell broke out. Well, you have been equipped to handle hell with no fear. The enemy has just been slammed with your Holy Spirit plan, and he is reacting to shut it down. He cannot stop it now. It is too late. But if he can get you to doubt the word of the Lord that led you here, then fear will drive you back. He wants to cause such a ruckus that you back down. But you need to stand strong now more than ever and use your authority to keep him in check.

Unfortunately, most of today's untrained Christians react to Satan's counterattack with surprise. They believe that since God has spoken to them and has given them His plan that everything is going to go smoothly and quickly with no surprises.

Now, do not misunderstand what I am saying. We have absolute authority over evil spirits, but we do not have absolute authority over people. It is to be noted that although I am under God's jurisdiction, many people around me are not and will fall prey to rumors and confusion. They may misjudge my motives or bring persecution against me.

But they cannot stop your Holy Spirit plan!!! The enemy will continue to come up a day late and a dollar short. God is way ahead of him and will lead you to your victory if you stay strong in faith and refuse to compromise.

The stepping out phase is the phase where it will take more

Week 47: Look for Opportunities

courage than faith to walk it out. Faith brought you to this moment, but now it will take courage to step out. I think the problem is that people get the Red Sea story and the Jordan River story confused.

In the Red Sea story, the people of Israel have been delivered out of Egypt and have traveled to the Red Sea where they appear to be hemmed in by the sea and mountains as Pharaoh has changed his mind and is coming after them. It seems there is no way of escape. But Moses raises his staff (authority), and the Red Sea parts. They cross over on dry land, and Pharaoh's army tries to follow. But as Pharaoh's army does so, the sea engulfs them, killing all of them. Israel is now free from Egypt and free from slavery. This is a mighty act of deliverance, and we all love to sing of God's deliverance.

Ahead is their promise, the land of Canaan. It is the land of their forefathers and has been promised to Abraham's seed. As they travel through the desert, the words of Moses ring in their ears: It will be a land that flows with milk and honey. It sounds too good to be true to the people who have only known slavery their entire lives. But there is a problem. The land is already occupied by other nations. As they approach the River Jordan, Moses decides to send out spies to check the best route for them to travel once they cross over into the new land and to bring back some of its fruit to prove to the people that it is a good land full of potential.

But the spies bring back a story that makes the nation of Israel want to head back to Egypt. The Israelites weep with discouragement and turn on God and Moses, thinking they have been lied to. Because of their unbelief, God does not lead them into the promise as He knows that without faith, they will be destroyed. That generation lives and dies in the desert until none of that generation is left.

Now, Joshua is commanded by God to lead them across. But again, as they come to the Jordan River, there is a problem. The river is at the flood stage, and the people cannot cross the fast-moving water. But once more, God splits the waters, and the Israelites walk across on dry land—this time not from conflict, as it was when they left Egypt, but into conflict as they prepare to capture their promise. This is what you must know. There could be issues or problems to solve as you step out, but do not fear. God will help you and protect you as you do. Always remember that right behind that problem is the promise. Never forget that.

Be problem conscious. Look for an opportunity.

—Your Financial Revolution: The Power of Provision

Week 47: Look for Opportunities

Prayer Focus

Thank God for giving you the ability to produce wealth and for the Holy Spirit providing you with solutions to problems so that you can be propelled to new places of responsibility.

Think on It

→ Do you tend to see mostly problems or mostly solutions in everyday life?

→ Have you ever just waited for God to somehow bring you money?

→ How can you be someone's solution right now?

Pursue Change

As long as there are problems to be solved, you are assured of having as many opportunities for promotion and increased income as you want.

This week, write down a list of any problems you encounter. Do others have the same problem you have seen? Can you see a solution to any of them? Think on it. That solution just may be your way of producing wealth.

Notes

Notes

Week 48

Stay Alert

Week 48: Stay Alert

I urge you, brothers and sisters, to watch out for those who cause divisions and put obstacles in your way that are contrary to the teaching you have learned. Keep away from them.
—Romans 16:17

"Don't be ignorant of Satan's schemes. See 1 Peter 5:8. Resist him with steadfast faith."

— *Nasty Gets Us Nowhere*

Accusation is one of the strategies Satan uses in an effort to create division... A stream of accusatory thoughts try to bombard all of our minds. And if he can't get us to receive his condemnation, he'll try to get us to condemn others. Just as he tried to divide heaven, the enemy seeks to divide the house of God and divide families. Satan knows a house divided cannot stand but will fall. He knows he must first tie us up before he can rob us. (See Mark 3:27.) That's why unity in a marriage, business, ministry, or family, coupled with submission to the spiritual authority that God has sanctioned, is crucial to resist the enemy's attacks and win in life.

Satan wants to divide our hearts, our families, and our spheres of influence. A spirit of division can open doors to him without God's covenant to protect us. It works to magnify our differences, to incite disgust or hatred between genders, ethnicities, leaders, and followers. Satan wants to stop God's increase in our lives, and he does so with divisiveness and unforgiveness. He wiggles a little seed of doubt into our minds and hearts to get us out of agreement with the Word of God, or out of agreement with our spouses and the body of Christ.

Don't be ignorant of Satan's schemes! You are in a battle, but Satan cannot control you outside of your will, without your cooperation and consent. You must first recognize that you are in a battle. Many people choose not to believe that—some even deny that Satan exists—but it's true. Your unwillingness to engage in battle with Satan doesn't mean

Week 48: Stay Alert

that the battle isn't raging; it just means you may lose. Once you realize the battle is real, you can learn to recognize what's going on and take the proper action to fight and transform the situation.

We can see Satan's scheme to discourage, divide, and uproot believers illustrated in the lives of Barnabas and Paul. Barnabas and Paul began to travel and preach the Good News of the Gospel. They met a Jewish sorcerer and false prophet. The governor wanted to hear the Word of God, but Bar-Jesus (also called Elymas) urged him not to listen. I love the incredible scene that played out next:

> *Saul, who was also called Paul, filled with the Holy Spirit, looked straight at Elymas and said, "You are a child of the devil and an enemy of everything that is right! You are full of all kinds of deceit and trickery. Will you never stop perverting the right ways of the Lord? Now the hand of the Lord is against you. You are going to be blind for a time, not even able to see the light of the sun." Immediately mist and darkness came over him, and he groped about, seeking someone to lead him by the hand. When the proconsul saw what had happened, he believed, for he was amazed at the teaching about the Lord.*
> —Acts 13:9-12

After this, the two sailed to Turkey, where nearly the whole city came to hear them preach the word of God.

What happens next doesn't surprise me. Satan doubled down on his counterattack. When you are gaining territory in the Kingdom, Satan sends offense and division to try to discourage you.

> *When the Jews saw the crowds, they were filled with jealousy. They began to contradict what Paul was saying and heaped abuse on him. Then Paul and Barnabas answered them boldly: "We had to speak the word of God to you first. Since you reject it and do not consider yourselves worthy of eternal life, we now turn to the Gentiles. For this is what the Lord has commanded us: 'I have made you a light for the Gentiles, that you may bring salvation to the ends of the earth.'"*
>
> *When the Gentiles heard this, they were glad and honored the word of the Lord; and all who were appointed for eternal life believed. The word of the Lord spread through the whole region. But the Jewish leaders incited the God-fearing women of high standing and the leading men of the city. They stirred up persecution against Paul and Barnabas, and expelled them from their region. So they shook the dust off their feet as a warning to them and went to Iconium. And the disciples were filled with joy and with the Holy Spirit.*
>
> —Acts 13:45-52

Week 48: Stay Alert

Paul and Barnabas could have spent all of their time dealing with the offenses of the Jews. They could have gotten discouraged. Instead, they kept their focus on their mission and continued to take territory for the Kingdom of God. That's how we have to be when dealing with division, strife, and offense.

—*Nasty Gets Us Nowhere*

Prayer Focus

Praise God that He has given you His full armor so you can stand against the devil's schemes (Ephesians 6).

Think on It

→ In what ways do you recognize the enemy comes against you most when you are taking territory for the Kingdom of God?

→ How do you keep from becoming discouraged when you feel attacked?

Pursue Change

This week, meditate daily on Ephesians 6:11-18a:

Put on the full armor of God, so that you can take your stand against the devil's schemes. For our struggle is not against flesh and blood, but against the rulers, against the authorities, against the powers of this dark world and against the spiritual forces of evil in the heavenly realms.

Therefore put on the full armor of God, so that when the day of evil comes, you may be able to stand your ground, and after you have done everything, to stand. Stand firm then, with the belt of truth buckled around your waist, with the breastplate of righteousness in place, and with your feet fitted with the readiness that comes from the gospel of peace.

In addition to all this, take up the shield of faith, with which you can extinguish all the flaming arrows of the evil one. Take the helmet of salvation and the sword of the Spirit, which is the word of God.

And pray in the Spirit on all occasions with all kinds of prayers and requests. With this in mind, be alert!

Week 48: Stay Alert

Pursue Change

Know this: The enemy has nothing on you, even if he's tried to trick you into thinking he does. God's grace is sufficient for you to deal with the enemy. Maintain that cloak of grace. Don't let the enemy get you out of agreement with heaven. Renew your mind and think the thoughts of God. Realize the authority you have. Go put your armor on.

Notes

Week 49

Set the Measure with a Big Vision

"Do not let fear speak to you when you are sowing and setting your measure. Be bold."

— *Your Financial Revolution: The Power of Generosity*

There is a great story with so much Kingdom revelation in it in 2 Kings 4:1-7.

This woman goes to the prophet for help. She is in debt and about to lose her sons. But interestingly enough, the prophet does not pull money out of his treasury. Instead, he asks her a very strange question in light of the circumstances: "What do you have in your house?"

You can almost hear her surprise in how she answers. "I have nothing at all!" she said. She adds the "at all" for emphasis. But she does mention what she does have. It's not much, but she has a small amount of olive oil. That is all the prophet needed to hear. That was the answer.

Elisha said, "Go around and ask all your neighbors for empty jars."

She left him and shut the door behind her and her sons. They brought the jars to her, and she kept pouring. When all the jars were full, she said to her son, "Bring me another one." But he replied, "There is not a jar left." Then the oil stopped flowing.

Note when the oil stopped flowing—not at a specified number of jars but when she ran out of jars. When all the jars were full, she told her son to bring her another one, and he said there was not a jar left. I'm sure she would have liked it to continue, but she had only gathered so many jars. Her

Week 49: Set the Measure with a Big Vision

increase was capped not by God but by her own thinking.

I am sure she probably wished she would have had more jars, many more jars. And if she really understood what was about to happen, I am sure she would have knocked on every door in town looking for jars. She might have even sent requests out to other cities to gather jars. The story had a good outcome though—her debts were paid, and the family lived on what was left after they sold the oil.

But what could the outcome have been? She could have paid off the debt of everyone that she knew, built a new town square, and helped so many people.

I believe if she had gathered a thousand jars, they would have all been filled. She set the measure!

God gives all of us the same opportunity that the woman had. We all must choose how we want to set the measure.

We all love to quote the first part of Luke 6:38—that if we give, we will reap with running over abundance. But many times, we fail to read the last part, the part that says we will only reap according to the same measure that we use in giving.

Why is this principle so vital? Well, let me give an example.

Let's say you are a beginning farmer and I tell you that I

want to purchase 5,000 bushels of wheat. You and I agree on a price per bushel, and you prepare to plant your 10-acre field with wheat for the harvest.

I think you know what will happen. You will fall terribly short in the bushels needed to fulfill our contract. Why? Because you have no idea how many acres it takes to harvest 5,000 bushels of wheat.

HOW MANY CHRISTIANS ARE LINING UP TRUCKS PREPARING TO TAKE THEIR HARVESTS TO MARKET BUT HAVE ONLY PLANTED TWO TOMATO PLANTS?

The measure in the farmer's example is the number of acres he planted. In the woman's case, it was the number of jars she gathered. In Jesus's example, it is the amount that we sow.

So, if the harvest we are expecting is not possible with the measure we set to receive it, then we have disappointment, and possibly people of little understanding could even blame God for what appears to be a failure of His Word.

When Peter gave his boat to Jesus to use that day on the lake, we saw that James and John's boat filled up with the exact harvest that Peter's faith had brought in because they were partners. But let me ask you this: If Peter had 1,000 boats that day in his business, how many boats would have filled up? If you said 1,000, you're correct. Again, we see

Week 49: Set the Measure with a Big Vision

the measure being set. The measure given is the container that God can fill. So, I encourage you to set the measure with a big vision.

—*Your Financial Revolution: The Power of Generosity*

Prayer Focus

Thank God for giving you the opportunity to set the measure. Ask Him to show you how to set the measure each time you give and to help you prepare for an abundant harvest.

Think on It

→ How does this excerpt from *Your Financial Revolution: The Power of Generosity* change how you think about receiving from God?

→ Have you ever asked God about a disappointment in your life?

→ Do you have a standard amount you give, or do you ask God what you should give?

Pursue Change

This week, meditate on Luke 6:38 and ask God to give you more understanding of the measure so you can set the measure with a big vision.

Give, and it will be given to you. A good measure, pressed down, shaken together and running over, will be poured into your lap. For with the measure you use, it will be measured to you.

—Luke 6:38

Notes

Notes

Week 50

Fight the Good Fight

Peace I leave with you; my peace I give you. I do not give to you as the world gives. Do not let your hearts be troubled and do not be afraid.

—John 14:27

"Our trust must be firmly planted in the purpose God gave us: to continue to answer the heavenly vision to build, to take territory, to possess all His promises in our work and lives, and to fight for a heavenly cause!"

— *Shark Proof*

Nehemiah was moved to rebuild the walls of Jerusalem. Nehemiah had wept when he heard about the devastation of Jerusalem and the broken walls of the once great city. He secured a release from his employer, King Artaxerxes, to go, with a blessing, to rebuild Jerusalem's walls.

It's not just important to have a heart for the vision and confirmation. It's just as important in the execution of the vision to share it with others who can come alongside you and share in the vision. As God instructed us, we were not sharing the vision for various reasons, but none of them were good. Nehemiah traveled to Jerusalem and shared the vision with the Israelites. *"I also told them about the gracious hand of my God on me and what the king had said to me. They replied, 'Let us start rebuilding.' So they began this good work"* (Nehemiah 2:18).

As Nehemiah did this, contenders and accusers appeared during the work to stop him and his team. Nehemiah, now challenged, had to fight both the enemies of his efforts and rebuild the walls. Winston Churchill fought the overwhelming voice of his own party that demanded he surrender Britain to Hitler. In the midst of this great opposition, he developed a plan to call upon his own people to surrender their boating vessels to remove the trapped British forces and save them from destruction. Nehemiah's plan succeeded, and so did Churchill's, but not without a fight.

Week 50: Fight the Good Fight

"I know the plans I have for you," says the Lord, "to bless you, not to harm you, and to bring you to a good end." God has a good end to any endeavor He has asked of you, but to be sure, anything worth doing will be met with some opposition. Surrendering is not an option we can afford. Too much is at stake! Opposition is not the proof you've missed God; it is almost always the guarantee you're onto something that hits His mark.

"You have been called into the Kingdom for such a time as this" is a phrase we have heard very often, but are we engaging in this calling? You can be sure that if God is calling, Satan is countering. But greater is He that is in you than He that is in the world. It's imperative that we don't let sharks stop the rebuilding and advancing of God's work in the earth. Whatever parts you or I have to play in that calling, we are all called to do our parts if Jesus is our Lord. Every man, woman, and child has some part to play in the Kingdom, and now is that time. It's important that we have laser focus on "advancing the Kingdom of God that revolutionizes lives."

Who or what will you allow to waylay you or cause you to stop fighting the good fight of faith? It's a good fight because it is the fight between good and evil, a fight of the ages to either obey God and His way or to let evil have its way with the lives of people.

Nehemiah succeeded with the rebuilding of the wall by

utilizing important principles that we need to examine to deal with difficult people. The tactics of shark warfare are evident in his story. I recognize these tactics that have been used against us, too, schemes that in past days caused us to be reticent to confidently share our calling and ask others to join us to build.

Maybe these tactics are working to stop you from your destiny at this very moment. The attack against God's plan on Nehemiah's life (and on each of us) took these forms:

1. Ridicule and mockery
2. False accusations
3. Distractions
4. Discouragement

The enemies of Nehemiah mocked him and made fun of his mission. The goal of mockery is to intimidate us into thinking thoughts like these: *How foolish of me to believe that this could actually happen for me! Maybe I missed God! I don't have what it takes to succeed at this!* The ultimate goal of all of these strategies is to get you to quit! Make no mistake: If you don't understand what's going on with these strategies, you may actually surrender to the enemy when victory is so close.

—Shark Proof

Week 50: Fight the Good Fight

Prayer Focus

Thank God that you have been called into the Kingdom for such a time as this (Esther 4:14) and that greater is He that is in you than he that is in the world (1 John 4:4). Ask Him to strengthen you to fight the good fight of faith and advance His work on the earth.

Think on It

→ Are you engaging in God's calling on your life right now? If so, how? If not, why?

→ What does it mean to you to "fight the good fight of faith"?

→ Which of the four types of attacks made on Nehemiah are most likely to get you to back down?

Pursue Change

This week, make a decision—you will not fret over the culture. You know that you're here for a reason. You have a mission and an assignment. This is why you're here.

God is in the people business, and we've got work to do.

Nehemiah 8:10 says, "*The joy of the Lord is your strength.*" When you feel like the pressure is on or you're under attack, get alone with God and tell Him what's on your mind; allow His presence to bring you joy and strengthen you for what lies ahead.

Notes

Notes

Week 51
Let Nothing Be Wasted

"Satisfied eats for today; the double portion builds a tomorrow!"

— *Your Financial Revolution: The Power of Rest*

Being satisfied is great, but it can lure you into a false sense of security. You need to look down the road a bit and know that what you just consumed will not be able to provide for what you need in a few hours. You will be hungry again. If you are only looking for the quick fix, the quick satisfaction of provision, you are going to miss the only thing that actually can change your life—the double portion.

When we all grew up in the earth curse financial system of painful toil and sweat, we dreamed of one thing, stopping! I mentioned this in a previous chapter. We did not dream of more work or another opportunity because, quite frankly, we were already overwhelmed with life and just holding out until the next vacation. Listen, the overwhelmed and "can't wait to stop" mindset is never going to take you anywhere. Even if an angel came into your bedroom and told you an idea from God, your mindset would still hold you back.

YOU MUST SEE PAST BEING SATISFIED TO CAPTURE THE DOUBLE PORTION!

Look at the story of feeding the 5,000 people from the book of John instead of the book of Mark.

> *Jesus then took the loaves, gave thanks, and distributed to those who were seated as much as they wanted. He did the same with the fish. When they had all had enough to eat, he said to his disciples,*

Week 51: Let Nothing Be Wasted

> *"Gather the pieces that are left over. Let nothing be wasted."*
>
> —John 6:11-12

In this version of the story, we see that it was Jesus who told them to go and gather the pieces, or fragments, and let nothing be wasted. I want you to get this. He had to tell them to do that because they did not see the opportunity. Put yourself in their shoes. You are full and satisfied, and all you want to do is to lie down and take a nap. Because of your earth curse training and your slavery mentality, when you are satisfied, it is time to stop. You see, the slave mentality works only when it has to, and when it doesn't have to, when it is satisfied, it stops. Jesus had to tell them to gather what was right in front of their eyes. The fragments were all around them on the ground, yet they made no effort to pick them up. But then again, in their minds, what were fragments worth anyway but to be left for the birds?

Jesus was trying to teach them something, something very important. He made a comment after He told them to gather the pieces, to let nothing be wasted! Everyone was full, everyone was satisfied, and no one wanted more bread and fish, well at least right then. But here is the problem—there is no Sabbath rest without gathering more than you need. When the Israelites gathered the manna on the sixth day, they were instructed to gather more than they needed. Them gathering more than they needed on that day became their provision on the seventh day, the day of rest. Jesus was teaching His disciples to look past being satisfied and to see the full provision of the Kingdom.

Although the disciples did not see the fragments until Jesus pointed them out, God had already given them the Sabbath rest, the double portion. They just did not see it. The Kingdom had already provided the food, multiplied the bread and fish, and fed all those people—but the Kingdom always supplies the double portion. God is never going to supply just satisfied; He will always supply more than enough.

Your measure, pressed down and shaken together, is your provision for that day. But Luke 6:38 goes on to say, "and running over!" The running over is the double portion. God always supplies the double portion, never just enough!!!! But if you were not aware of that, and the grain was running over, you might just let it fall to the ground as you were totally focused on the satisfied portion in front of you and not prepared to capture the overflow. In doing so, you would fail to capture and enjoy the double portion. But if you realized how the Kingdom operates, knew about and anticipated the full provision, you would be prepared to act and capture all that God provided.

—Your Financial Revolution: The Power of Rest

Week 51: Let Nothing Be Wasted

Prayer Focus

Thank God that He ALWAYS and freely provides more than enough—His double portion—as your loving Father, not based on what you do but on who you are in Christ!

Think on It

→ When was the last time you felt both mentally and physically rested?

→ What is a potential fragment in your life?

→ After reading this week's book excerpt, do you think you've gotten too comfortable with just being satisfied?

Pursue Change

This week, declare this personalized version of Isaiah 61:7-9 over your life:

> Instead of shame, I will receive a double portion, and instead of disgrace, I will rejoice in my inheritance—and so I will inherit a double portion in my land, and everlasting joy will be mine. For my Lord loves justice; He hates robbery and iniquity. In His faithfulness, He will reward me and make an everlasting covenant with me. My descendants will be known among the nations and my offspring among the peoples. All who see me will acknowledge that the Lord has blessed me.

Notes

_____
_____
_____
_____
_____

Notes

Week 52
Keep Your Peace

"Jesus modeled what's right for you, so model it for the culture. Shock them with peace and confidence that surpasses all understanding."

— *Better Than You Think*

YOUR PERSONAL REVOLUTION

Maintain peace in your life despite disrupting circumstances and conflicts.

1. Watch Out for Distractions.

> It's very easy to walk out life by the traditions that we're used to and to not keep our eyes on the Word of God. It doesn't take much to get us off. It doesn't take much to cause us to stumble.
>
> The culture is shocking. If you turn on the news, if you look around, you will hear and see things that don't look like what you see in the Word of God. The Bible talks about renewing your mind to the Word of God, but it can also be reversed. You can renew your mind to the shock of the culture…
>
> When you let the small things trip you up, you are renewing your mind to the culture and not the Word of God.
>
>> *The fruit of the Spirit is love, joy, peace, patience, kindness, goodness, faithfulness, gentleness and self-control. Against such things there is no law.*
>> —Galatians 5:22-23
>
> That's the fruit of God's Spirit, and yet that is not what we see in the world. Many times, that is not

Week 52: Keep Your Peace

what we see in our very own lives!

Are you modeling the fruit of the Spirit? Or are you feeding your spirit distractions?

2. Speak to the Problems.

We must speak to storms instead of letting them speak to us. What Jesus did (in Matthew 8:23-26) is what you and I need to do when we are in the midst of the storms we face in life. We need to know who we are, what we have, and that God protects us. We can stand up in the midst of a storm, and we can rebuke the wind and the waves.

The disciples had completely forgotten who was in the boat with them. They forgot the promises of God, but Jesus was promise focused. He immediately began to enact the promises of God by speaking the Word of God!

3. See Promises, Not Problems.

Jesus always saw something different than the rest of His companions. Instead of seeing problems, He saw promises. Jesus knew where His faith was and in whom He trusted.

When you see a problem that already has a solution,

do you waste time worrying about it? Do you lose sleep over it? Do you grow fearful and anxious over it? No!

God has already given you the answers to your problems and His promises for your life in His Word. Living life without taking advantage of God's promises is like taking a test without taking advantage of the study guide. Peace comes with answers. When you know there is already a solution to your problem, there is peace.

4. Be Bold.

When you move off of what the Word says, you become stagnant. You lose vision, grow anxious, fearful, discontent, and, ultimately, move your trust from God. You see what God says, but then you look at the circumstances.

Boldly fix your eyes on Jesus, and He will make a way.

I want to challenge you to be bold and to be courageous. There are big things inside of you. God's put something special in you that other people need. If you believe anything else, you're listening to the wrong thoughts and the wrong messages.

Week 52: Keep Your Peace

5. Know the Truth.

> If there is only one thing that you walk away from this book with, I hope it is the concept of renewing your mind. What you meditate on will produce itself in your life.
>
> You have to feed your spirit the truth! If you feed your spirit the world's thoughts and the world's fear, then that is what you are going to get in your life. But if you feed it the promise of God's perfect peace that surpasses all understanding, then you are going to enjoy the benefit of that!

6. Decide What You Believe.

> The only way the devil can stop you from the promise of God is if you believe lies. Take self-control, put it to work in your life, and say, "No, I'll not believe a lie." You have to be forceful about this. I'm telling you, this is a fight for your very life. You will become your thoughts. What you behold is what you become. What you believe is what you receive.
>
> You can't achieve success by reacting to your circumstances. You have to be deliberate, intentional, and steer toward your goal. If you don't decide what you believe, once again, you are like the ship that reacts to the waves—you will end up shipwrecked!

Meditate on the Word of God, align yourself with what the Bible says, and establish a firm foundation of what you believe.

—*Better Than You Think*

Prayer Focus

Thank God that He keeps you in perfect peace and that you have the perfect model of a peaceful life in Jesus.

Think on It

→ Do you consider yourself to be a peaceful person?

→ Does it take much to get your focus off of God? If not, why? If so, what needs to change?

→ When was the last time you lost sleep over a problem? What happened?

Pursue Change

If you spend your life *looking* for peace, you'll find yourself compromising *a lot*. What you need to realize is that you already have peace IN you. No matter what the circumstances are in your life, you have the kind of peace Jesus did—the kind that lets you sleep in the boat while the storm is going on.

Getting that peace requires that you become familiar with the Spirit of God. That takes prayer. You have to know when to step forward and when to step back. When you don't know what to do, you need to pray in the Spirit. The answers won't come by *your* strength or *your* wisdom. They will come by His.

This week, pray in the Spirit and talk to the person who IS peace—the Holy Spirit. He lives in you.

Notes